"Gail's quest is honest and authentic one's been taught. She's sought God ery and only good things can come fr~~~ ~~

—**Hesh Epstein**, Orthodox Rabbi

"I love reading stories of people coming to a life-giving faith. Especially when the hard and harsh things that comprise any life get full attention. Gail's is no glib testimony, but a moving, carefully unrolling narrative with flashes of humor and glimpses of insight. She confronts heartache and tough questions without flinching, all the while showing how God walked alongside her, and brought to her mercy and hope. Her story will stir something similarly satisfying and sustaining in others."

—**Timothy Jones**, Dean Trinity Episcopal Cathedral

"I read this book in one sitting. Coming myself from Jewish heritage, it stirred my heart and I found I couldn't put it down! Every Christian should understand the Jewish underpinnings of Christianity and this work lays them out beautifully. This book is both wonderfully theological and deeply personal. Gail is stunningly and authentically honest about her own journey, faith, and family. I found myself shedding tears of sadness and joy! You will find great wisdom here that may just change your life."

—**Alfred "Al" T. K. Zadig Jr.**, former Rector of All Saints Church in Chevy Chase, Maryland in the Diocese of Washington, DC

"Linda and I are spellbound about the way God used us in Gail's metamorphosis. Just as physical birth can entail a long and painful experience, so it was with Gail's spiritual rebirth. Our recent experience of reading her book was intensely emotional. Because the Jewish embrace of Jesus represents an earth-shattering change, I have not been able to contain my tears. Her writing, transparent and without guile, has well-placed, healing Scriptures that affect the reader like a balm on an open wound."

—**Glenn Welsford**, retired Presbyterian minister, PCA

"Gail Baker's *Matzah Balls to Communion Wafers* is a strikingly frank and unique assessment of her personal, social, and, ultimately, theological path. An emotional and intellectual treatment without veneer, it reflects the interplay between the Spirit's leading and an honest willed search."

—**Gerald Mills**, Senior Pastor, Providence Presbyterian Church, PCA

"Gail Baker has given us a powerful account of her personal spiritual pilgrimage that engages both the mind and heart and lights the way for all as we encounter the holy in the large and small experiences of our own lives. With searing honesty, profound insight and extraordinarily engaging vulnerability, Gail invites us to join her on a life quest for the truth of God. As her story progresses, we see how the unfolding mystery of Jesus Christ is revealed, known and trusted in the broken places, wounds, and hurts of life. It remains an account of irrepressible joy, gratitude and openness to the future. As she wrestles to understand her life and relationships, Gail weaves together a beautiful tapestry that draws from the best of Jewish and Christian scholars, theologians, artists and mystics. No one can read her writing without entering into an internal conversation about the meaning and purpose of one's own life before God."

—**Lewis F. Galloway**, retired Senior Pastor, Second Presbyterian Church, Indianapolis

"Gail's bold determination to seek truth in the face of strong opposition is a transformative model for all seekers. The depth of her spiritual journey authentically reflects the person Gail is. Like Nicodemus, she comes to Jesus in the night with difficult questions, and ends up at a garden tomb bearing spices, fearlessly trusting the promises of God's love."

—**Patricia C. Malanuk**, Trinity Episcopal Cathedral

"A beautifully written and provocative account of one woman's spiritual journey." Baker writes with a deeply felt spirituality, her prose, often, elegantly taking on the form of prayer: 'I continue to write so that I can better know what I feel and think about a matter. As a form of communication, it resembles prayer—reaching deep into my psyche and speaking to a subconscious part of my soul.' She artfully braids revealing, confessional memoir with thought-provoking reflections on the nature of her spirituality, which dwells in the convergence of mystical Judaism and Christianity. Her search for faith is a rigorously intellectual one, conducted through the meticulous study of not only the Bible, but also philosophy and theology.

Still her remembrance never devolved into arid, scholarly study. Her recollection is still powerfully moving and told with courage and self-effacing humor. With great nuance, Baker describes the profound consolation that she found in Christ as a Jewish woman, and in the process, she makes a valuable contribution to a deeper understanding of the Judeo-Christian tradition."

—Kirkus Review

"Genuinely affecting and revelatory, Gail Baker's candid memoir conveys a poignant story of her metamorphosis from Judaism to Christianity, one which traversed the craggy, psyche-borne territories of faith, suffering, and religious affiliation.

Delivering a touching, coherent and insightful work which speaks to the soul of the reader, author Baker shares her spiritual hardships and triumphs with grounded openness and grace, brimming not only with emotion, but with scholarly authenticity and insight.

When her search eventually brought her to the point of no return—crossing the impalpable barrier that separates Judaism and Christianity, Gail Baker became a hero and an inspiration. Not because she turned her back to Judaism, but because she bravely took charge of her faith, daring to step away from her Jewish culture, while seeking a more enriching relationship with God. *Matzah Balls to Communion Wafers: How a not-so Kosher Jewish Girl Fell in Love with Jesus,* made for a spiritually satisfying read that easily kept my attention. In particular, what immediately appealed to me about the overall narrative is the eloquence of Baker's writing style. Her words flow easily and stylishly, permeating the read with a poetic bent, both expressive and engaging. Moreover, her writing guides you through her experiences with a literate clarity that allows for a genuine author-reader connection."

—Pacific Book Review

"*Matzah Balls to Communion Wafers* recounts Gail's journey to marry her Jewish heritage to her newfound Christian faith. Her story will resonate with women—mothers, daughters, wives—as it details how her faith carried her through difficulties with her son, parents, and rejection from her community. I would recommend this book to any Christian who loves a good conversion story. I would also recommend the book to Christian-curious Jewish or agnostic people."

—Manhattan Book Review

"What is religion, if not a source of comfort, solace, and community? For Gail Baker, a proud Jewess raised in a predominantly Christian, and often bigoted, South Carolina, religion is complicated. As for many Jews, the theology of her Judaism is enmeshed with Jewish culture, history, commitment to social and civic participation, and in an identity that both included and transcended religious belief.

Baker's story of growing up honors her strong Jewish roots and values, her defiance during formative Christian proselytizing and anti-Semitic experiences, and her efforts to lead an honorable adult secular Jewish life. She describes, in excruciating candor, the later torment of raising a son who suffered debilitating depression and related troubles into adulthood, and how her need for guidance and comfort eventually leads her to seek out Jesus Christ.

This relatable tale of an all-too-human woman facing unspeakable sadness and seeking solace is a gut punch for any parent. But it's the body blow of guilt over appearing to abandon her people to collude with their persecutors that gives Baker the most concern. How she reconciles her intellectual understanding of Jewish experience with her emotional and spiritual attraction to Christianity makes for a heartfelt and often uncomfortably candid memoir.

Ultimately, though she faces her own questions and those of community members on both sides of the Bible, Baker makes her choice and her case, bringing with her the best of civic and community practice she formed as a Jew. Though she fears friends and family will judge her harshly, her ultimate choice of Christianity presents not as rejection of Judaism, nor as tacit approval of the ills done to Jews in the name of Christianity. Instead, she describes her conversion in a sympathetic and understandable light, as her embrace of the lifestyle that brought her the most joy, peace, and promise at a time in life when she needed it most."

—Tulsa Book Review

"*Matzah Balls to Communion Wafers: How a not-so-Kosher Jewish Girl Fell in Love with Jesus* by Gail Baker is the author's memoir of her life and journey on the path toward finding answers to questions surrounding her personal faith. With her identity as firmly grounded in Judaism as nearly every other facet of her life, Baker is forced to confront both internal resistance and fierce opposition from her family, community, and the ties that bind her to a faith. Ultimately, she finds a balance between the two that is as individual as it is inspirational.

Matzah Balls to Communion Wafers by Gail Baker is a wonderful book that will resonate with readers of all faiths, particularly those who have converted from one firm belief to another. There is a very human and authentic tone to Baker's writing, which feels so much like a friend sitting on the sofa with you, telling the story from the beginning of how she managed to make it there. The narrative is light and humorous when it's appropriate, without detracting from the heavy weight of her experience, and she's definitely a woman that's easy to connect with from the first page. I'd absolutely recommend this moving autobiography to anyone interested in real life interfaith coming of age stories, even when it occurs in their late 30's."

—Readers' Favorite Review

"*Matzah Balls to Communion Wafers* is an intriguing memoir written by Gail Baker detailing her own spiritual journey from Judaism to Christianity. A Jewish girl at heart, she grew up in the Bible Belt of Columbia, South Carolina in a secular Jewish family. Baker did not question her spirituality much until her son, Michael, at the age of 9, started having behavioral issues. Michael was dealing with depression, oppositional issues, an eating disorder, and, eventually, drug addiction. Afraid of the backlash from her Jewish community, she started secretly studying Christianity. She eventually found the love of God and the teachings of Christianity offered her the solace she needed. Gail Baker is clearly a gifted writer. She writes with such candidness, beauty, and eloquence, it's like reading poetry at times. In her writing, it is evident that she is very knowledgeable about Judaism and Christianity; she personally studied it intensively for years. I thoroughly enjoyed reading the stories relating to her upbringing, her family—the more personal aspect of her memoir."

—Seattle Book Review

"Baker chronicles her spiritual journey with a methodical, research-based approach. She eventually comes to the conclusion that she finds the most comfort in Christianity's approach to life's persistent woes. Baker's research is a veritable reading list for those who want answers about any grief, fear, guilt or doubt they may be experiencing in their life."

—San Francisco Book Review

Matzah Balls to Communion Wafers

Matzah Balls to Communion Wafers

How a Not-So-Kosher Jewish Girl Fell in Love with Jesus

Gail Baker

FOREWORD BY
Philip D. Yancey

RESOURCE *Publications* · Eugene, Oregon

MATZAH BALLS TO COMMUNION WAFERS
How a Not-So-Kosher Jewish Girl Fell in Love with Jesus

Resource Publications
An Imprint of Wipf and Stock Publishers
199 W. 8th Ave., Suite 3
Eugene, OR 97401

www.wipfandstock.com

PAPERBACK ISBN: 978-1-5326-8204-9
HARDCOVER ISBN: 978-1-5326-8205-6
EBOOK ISBN: 978-1-5326-8206-3

Manufactured in the U.S.A.

Dedication

Once in a lifetime, heaven willing, God puts in our midst a person so spirit-filled, steadfast, and stellar that faith becomes known not through words but through example.

I dedicate this chronicle to Marie Pricilla Pugh, one who lived life on such a level that everyone around her saw new possibilities of trust and surrender.

Even if I could adequately describe her character, I fear my words would dispel the mystery.

Responding to circumstances that might break another, she would voice a familiar refrain: "Well, all I can do is pray."

At the end of a life fraught with turbulence, her luminous eyes peering into mine, she said "Gail, God has been so good to me." Indeed, he had.

Her unfathomable assurance of God's love will, forever, pique my imagination and lay waste the familiar rhythms of my mundane soul.

To God be the glory.

In memoriam, Ken Walden, 1948–2018

Contents

CONTENTS

Foreword

I READ THIS BOOK on a trip to Eastern Europe. In Belarus I visited a pit where, in 1942, Nazi soldiers lined up five thousand Jews from the Minsk ghetto and shot them, in plain view in the center of the city. In Hungary I toured the largest synagogue in Europe, mostly empty now after the extermination of half a million Jews. During one two-month period, twelve thousand Hungarian Jews per day arrived at Auschwitz in cattle cars, destined for the crematoriums. Winston Churchill said, "There is no doubt that this persecution of Jews in Hungary and their expulsion from enemy territory is probably the greatest and most horrible crime ever committed in the whole history of the world."[1]

I am still haunted by my visit to Babi Yar, a grassy ravine in Kiev, Ukraine. Now a memorial park, this peaceful setting was the site of Hitler's first large-scale massacre of Jews. The entire Jewish population of Kiev was ordered to report with their belongings and warm clothes to a train station, from which they would be transported to a better place for resettlement. Instead, soldiers herded them behind barbed wire and stripped them of all their belongings, including clothes. Divided into groups of ten, the Jews, naked and terrified, were marched to the side of the ravine, and machine-gunned. The killing went on from morning to night for two days: twenty-two thousand died the first day and twelve thousand the second. German guards strode atop the bodies in the gully and shot in the neck any who showed signs of life.

On this trip, and on others to such places as Auschwitz, Dachau, and Bergen-Belsen, I have confronted the long history of animosity toward the Jewish people. The Holocaust has become our central metaphor for evil, but it was only the most dramatic eruption of history's pattern of hatred and persecution directed against the Jews.

1. https://www.nytimes.com/1981/10/04/books/the-hungarian-episode.html

Shylock, in Shakespeare's *The Merchant of Venice*, voiced his bewilderment:

> Hath not a Jew eyes? Hath not a Jew hands, organs, dimensions, senses, affections, passions? Fed with the same food, hurt with the same weapons, subject to the same diseases, healed by the same means, warmed and cooled by the same winter and summer as a Christian is? If you prick us, do we not bleed? If you tickle us, do we not laugh? If you poison us, do we not die, and if you wrong us, shall we not seek revenge?[2]

Anti-Semitism is especially grievous among Christians, for we share the same theological heritage. "Inside every Christian is a Jew," Pope Francis has said. Both groups accept the Hebrew Bible as a revelation from God. Indeed, for the first few decades Christian converts were expected to follow Levitical laws governing such matters as circumcision and kosher foods. The book of Acts and Paul's letters detail the controversy that arose when Christians chose a different path.

I marvel that, in view of our violent history, any Jew would convert to Christianity (just as I marvel that so many African-American slaves adopted the Christian faith of their owners). Gail Baker has given us a step-by-step account of what the journey involves for a modern Jew who decides to follow Jesus. Hers is no blinding-light conversion story, but rather a process spanning years of struggle and anguish, years that echo twenty centuries of misunderstanding between Christians and Jews. She writes, "Exploring ultimate issues opened my eyes to the innocent suffering at the center of the universe. An anguish that could have destroyed me became a portal into a realm with the only voice capable of stilling it."

All the while, a tangled subplot has been unfolding in the background. Gail's Jewish family and community are scandalized, her husband is perplexed, and her son who suffers from depression and an eating disorder goes on to develop an addiction to cocaine. Throughout the years of his healing, her faith enables her to let go of pessimism and live a life tempered with gratitude.

Gail recounts her own bafflement over anti-Semitism. How to explain it? One by one, she examines key doctrines—the nature of God, Jesus' divinity, the problem of evil, the Trinity, atonement—and describes how she has come to terms with each. She ultimately yields, not to one single illumination, but to many incremental points of light. In a final act of surrender

2. *The Merchant of Venice*, Scene III, act i.

she prays, "I'm sorry you had to go through so much in proving yourself to me. I am yours forever—and, as fair warning, I am high maintenance."

The novelist Walker Percy used to say that the story behind his faith could be expressed in four words: God, Jews, Jesus, church. In a memoir both intellectual and personal, Gail has accepted the challenge of linking together those four words.

The biblical prophets speak of Israel becoming a blessing to the whole world, a light to the gentiles. The theologian Jürgen Moltmann has pointed out that Israel's "no" to Jesus had an unintended consequence. "Without Israel's 'no' the Christian church would have remained an inner-Jewish messianic revival movement. But because of the Jewish 'no,' the Christian community had a surprising experience. It discovered that the Spirit of God comes upon Gentiles so that they are seized by faith in Christ directly, without becoming Jews first of all."[3]

In her tortuous quest, Gail learned that not all Jews said "no" to Jesus. As she told her family, "I am the very person you knew so many years ago. I do not worship the church or other Christians. I worship a rabbi who cried over Jerusalem and who lived and died a Jew. I have not gone over to the other side—rather, Jesus is one of us."

Philip D. Yancey

3. https://www.religion-online.org/article/israels-no-jews-and-jesus-in-an-unredeemed-world/

Preface

LEST THE READER EXPECT a precipitous dazzling conversion story, I give caveats as fair warning. Having spent a lifetime immersed in the values and sensibilities of a close-knit Jewish community, I understand the agitation when a Jew leaves the fold. Some rightly ask, "How could a Jew possibly betray the memory of countless souls who preferred death to conversion at the point a sword?"

Over the years my faith was incubating, I agonized over such identity conundrums. Mired in uncertainty and vacillation, the temptation to leave faith aside was at least as great as the will to move forward.

I, finally, attained solace by relying on intuitive prayer rather than common sense or logic. Mystics throughout the ages solved paradoxical puzzles, or koans, by opening up their imagination in this way. Surrendering my quandary to God allowed me to rest in the mystery of what he, alone, could know. Only when I relinquished control in this way, did the pieces of the Christian spiritual puzzle fall into place with uncanny lucidity.

Reflecting, further, on how I overcame my doubts, I see a pattern of dissonance and renegotiation. I will always understand the Jewish mindset—that of a minority group trying to protect itself. Paradoxically, as I contemplated leaving a civilization always on the edge of survival, pride in my identity became strengthened and chiseled, honed as if on a rough-edged stone. Without pretense, I can state that the Jewish mystique, in its timeless unfolding within the bloodstream of history, is writ large upon my psyche.

Though I see my epiphany as a seamless progression of my overall values and disposition, for certain loved ones, my new direction remains a complete anomaly. I took to writing as a means to bridge this gap. When I, first, told my parents of my belief, they reacted with swift antagonism. I remember Dad's telling remark: "At least, if you were younger, I could put you over my knee and spank you." At thirty-seven, I had insulted my family and the memory of generations who preceded me.

Looking back, I can clearly see my grandparents' faces. Sadly, they may see mine as one obscured by anti-Semitism, violence, and misconceptions. Though I understand why the mere mention of Jesus would cause them to bristle, I long to tell them: "I am the very same person you knew so many years ago. I do not worship the church or other Christians. I worship a rabbi who cried over Jerusalem and who lived and died a Jew. I have not gone over to the other side—rather, Jesus is one of us."

Examining the past resembles dismantling the foundation of a long-standing house. Only from the vantage point of seventy, have I been able to credibly reassemble the building blocks. Henry David Thoreau, analyzing the pitfalls of autobiography, suggested that a writer such as myself, resembles someone looking back to see his shadow. The head, the most rational part, can never be viewed in its entirety. In a similar vein, I find it difficult to separate the most important elements of my journey from the overall backdrop of my life. Like the forest for the trees, my very omissions may speak volumes. One thing remains certain: God used the best and worst of my life to weave a tapestry foreshadowing spiritual renewal.

The uniqueness of my story derives from the fact that I am the "unexpected Christian," the kind that religious people have a hard time with. Yet, this is the very kind Jesus draws in, time and again, in the Gospel accounts. As a liberal Jew living in the Bible Belt, I had difficulty forging a faith of my own apart from cultural war stereotypes. Over time, taking on the label, "a congregation of one," I considered my situation to be an indication of God's sense of humor.

If living on the boundaries of two cultures is grist for the mill, I trust that I've gained a creative edge. At the very least, I understand the power of words, and how a certain turn of phrase can either afflict or heal. As writing serves to clarify, I can distill the issue of conversion down to a single salient point: When the story of Jesus is framed in the context of leaving one's tradition, very few Jews will consider it. When it becomes framed in the context of a loving God who takes on the pain of all who suffer innocently, the paradigm shifts from one of tradition to that of truth.

Leaving a path inhabited by yesterdays buried deep, I held fast to the classic Jewish notion that suffering never signifies God's last word. As vestigial memory, the idea became a single unifying strand, enabling me to assimilate Judaism and Christianity into a coherent whole.

The Jewish Orthodox New Testament scholar, Pinchas Lapide, while affirming the historical truth of the resurrection, did not hold to the messiahship of Jesus. In *Encountering Jesus—Encountering Judaism,* Lapide described the resurrection as the most Jewish part of the New Testament. As God's final word in redemptive suffering, it symbolizes the quintessence of hope which allowed the Jewish faith to flourish over centuries of persecution.

In the sense of coming full circle, I can relate to the words of T. S. Elliot:

> We shall not cease from exploration
>
> And the end of all our exploring
>
> Will be to arrive where we started
>
> And know the place for the first time.
>
> Through the unknown, remembered gate
>
> When the last of earth left to discover
>
> Is that which was the beginning.[4]

I tread carefully in describing the nature of faith. Even to juggle shopworn and stale language around it risks trivializing something that defies close countenance or introspection. If we read to stave off loneliness, I trust that my words, familiar as they are to me, have the potential to embolden those who've encountered what Shakespeare termed "the slings and arrows of outrageous fortune."[5] As readers engage with me and identify with my paradoxical and, often, challenging path, they will see how the Christian message answers the deep yearning within each of us to resolve human suffering.

---

4. Eliot, "Giddings," 59.

5. *Hamlet*, Act III, scene i.

Acknowledgements

First and foremost, I wish to thank my son Michael for allowing me to write about him. I frame his difficulties around a single event occurring in his childhood rather than the totality of his life. I trust that his bravery and fortitude will encourage all who seek to overcome the effects of trauma.

I could not have completed this project without the unfailing support of my husband Steve. His resilience and humor have served to offset life's harsher realities. His many acts of unselfish devotion continue to enliven my days and boost my spirit.

My deepest appreciation goes to my phenomenal sister, Laurie Walden, whose prayers and editing skills helped bring this book to fruition. Her love and generosity of spirit allow me to state that she is my soulmate and best friend.

My prayerful relationship with Lillian Ginn and Gaye Whitmire has afforded me the life-sustaining fellowship crucial to my walk. Their passion for this project was the impetus for its completion. Their devotion has made the love of Jesus a tangible reality.

I wish to thank Philip Yancey whose books played a seminal role in my conversion. As both mentor and friend, he has provided invaluable counsel and encouragement. I'm certain that without his endorsement, my chronical would have never landed a spot the marketplace.

Many thanks to my agent David Shepherd of DRS Agency who risked taking me on as a virtual unknown. I benefitted greatly from the creativity and wisdom of the editors at Wipf and Stock.

A huge debt of gratitude also goes to Cascadia Author Services, Mary Cartledge Hayes, and my exceedingly talented writing coach and editor, Susan Levi Wallach. I also wish to thank Cole Connor at Apollo's Bow for his technical expertise in social media.

ACKNOWLEDGEMENTS

Many thanks to my sisters in the Ark group at Trinity Episcopal Cathedral. Their friendship has made church a veritable homeland for my soul.

I am eternally grateful to Dr. Philip Steude and Amy Montanez whose psychological and spiritual counsel has stood me in good stead over many years.

Special thanks are due to the following friends who were kind enough to read my manuscript and offer suggestions: Patty and Vinny Covino, Judy Tighe, Suzie Fields, Steve and Sarah Nakrosis, Canon Patsy Malanuk, Dean Timothy Jones, Dr. Lewis Galloway, Dr. Gerald Mills, Rev. T. K. Zadig, Rabbi Hesh Epstein, Adrienne Bellinger, Keith Bapcock, Linda LeSourd Lader, Dr. Chaya Stoneberg, Rev. George Crowe, Glenn and Linda Welsford, Father Philip Whitehead, Dr. Michael Kogan, Penni Nadel, Peggy Jacobs, Cyd Berry, Carla Davis, Georgia Marshall, and Jack Kurtz.

CHAPTER 1

Setting the Stage: An Imperfect Life

By the time I reached middle school, I'd had my fill of Christians and Christianity. Growing up in Columbia, South Carolina, I was often targeted for conversion. The last unfortunate episode occurred when a male friend returned home with me after a date.

Sitting in my driveway in his new ruby-red Ford Mustang, I took in the aroma of new leather and peered at the high-tech widgets on the dash. I said, "Congratulations, Bill. The seats are just gorgeous—so soft and luxurious."

He tried to hide his peacock pride by pursing his lips, then said, "Yeah, I think I'll keep this one better than the last. Anyway, I'm glad you like it." After a long pause, he cleared his throat and stammered, "Gail, I need to talk to you about something serious. I've known you for a long time, and you know how much I care, so I'll just come right out and say it."

Looking at him curiously, I asked, "Bill, what in the world is it?"

He said, "Well, it's about your salvation."

An immediate barrier came between us, and I snarled, "I just can't believe you!"

Defensively, he said, "I know how much Judaism means to you and your family, but the fact is, if you died tomorrow, Gail, you would burn in hell."

I saw no tears of genuine agony over my supposed destiny. To make matters worse, he belonged to Forest Lake Country Club, at the time a bastion of anti-Semitism and elitism. Usually, I stopped these conversations short, but this time I took a different approach.

"Listen, do you believe Jesus is coming back?" I asked.

"Yes, of course, I do," he said.

"Do you think he could come back next week or next month?" I asked.

"Well, yes. He told us to expect him, any time, but what's your point?" he asked.

"Do you realize that if he comes soon, he couldn't even dampen the backdoor of your country club? Bill, I think you're missing something here. Jesus was Jewish," I said.

He blurted, "Well if that's true, he must have converted. I'm not stupid, Gail. I know Jesus was a Christian."

"No," I said emphatically. "In fact, Jesus remained a Jew until the day he died. What's more, his followers were Jews, too. You may have even heard of them—Matthew, Mark, and John. But don't worry, Bill—you wouldn't recognize Jesus if he stared you right in the face. He'd look more like Yasser Arafat than that blasted blond picture on your Sunday School wall."

His face blanched, and his eyes glazed over. Ignoring any semblance of church-like decorum, he raged, "Dammit, Gail, you don't know what the hell you're talking about."

I wasted no time getting out of his car. He slammed his foot on the accelerator and sped away faster than I could say Jesus Christ. I heard his tires screech several blocks away, sure that I'd never have any trouble with him again.

I have always abhorred a theology that has God saying, "If you don't love me, I will torture you." My knowledge of the church's history of forced conversions gave the word proselytize an evil ring. I could never understand how a person's nominal acceptance of Jesus, something akin to choosing the right door at the fun fair, could serve as a litmus test for heaven. Wanting no part of a God who devalued freedom of conscience, I grew up convinced of a huge divide between Christian and Jewish values.

Eighteen years later, certain dire circumstances forced me to consider something that my rational mind could never have foreseen or imagined. Happily married to my husband, Steve, I was drawn into an emotional maelstrom that forced me to reconsider my assumptions about Christians and Christianity. When this new reality peaked, I had no way to unsee it and no way to turn back.

On a rainy Thursday afternoon, I found myself walking toward the back entrance of our neighborhood mall. As I carefully adjusted my hood to disguise my profile, I watched the last vestige of fall color: vermilion, rust, and yellow leaves dance and swirl their way to the ground. Inside, I made my way through the crowds. Then, as though it happened every day, I crossed the threshold of my first Christian bookstore.

The store had the appearance of a cheerful Hallmark card shop, with signs indicating directions—Bibles, devotionals, commentaries, biographies, and guides to moral living. I saw sections with such labels as "Steps to Salvation," "The Four Spiritual Laws," and "How to Find Peace with God." These simplistic notions flew in the face of my secular, analytical upbringing. Having recently studied the Holocaust, I had little tolerance for tidy resolutions about who deserved heaven or hell. Though I felt safe from prying eyes, technically I should have worn special gear or a breastplate of armor—such was the nature of the spiritual battle I had just commenced.

A year prior to this, our son, Michael, showed signs of depression and serious emotional problems. The sudden onset of insidious, impossible-to-manage symptoms confounded Steve and me. Michael's attitude turned sullen and belligerent, and he refused to do his chores, complete homework, or comply with school rules. A mysterious force had changed our lovely boy into someone hardly recognizable. Over the years, these difficulties steamrolled into an eating disorder and drug addiction.

His depression caused my healthy motherly love to devolve into disabling enmeshment. The atmosphere surrounding his profound sadness became my quiet obsession. Dark melancholia permeated my very marrow, rendering me practically senseless. In my over-involved state, I believed that I could detect his mood by the tone and color of his skin. I marked every nuance of his eyes as they fixated on an unknown and unfathomable realm.

My poignant bittersweet love for Michael forced me through a tunnel to the outer edges of reality. With eyes shut tight and breath suspended, I emerged from the chaos unscathed, trying to discern just how I managed to survive. As it happened, God ruled over the lesser light of night.

Though he received professional help, his problems lingered. I felt helpless and guilt-ridden every time I got negative feedback from teachers and other mothers. Acutely aware of the fragility of life, I lived in constant fear of great trouble around the corner. Though at first my emotions bordered on hysteria, they soon became submerged beneath the surface in a glacier-like realm. Constant worry left me in a state of blind resignation. Over time, when the swell in my heart and the lump in my throat disappeared, I found myself going through the motions of life, a ghostly figure skulking.

The First Day: Spirit's Peaking

The morning began when sirens jarred me out of a sound sleep. Their foreboding shrills, like birds of prey, hovered closer and closer before stopping at a house nearby. I heard the faint sound of weeping, sharp voices shouting directions, and then the slow thrum of the ambulance idling back onto the street and into the dark.

Looking outside the bedroom window, I could barely detect our newly planted birch trees. A burst of air from the windowsill indicated another frigid day, so I tucked the comforter snugly around Steve who still slept soundly.

Whatever the outcome of the emergency, my neighbors would have wounds from the aftermath. My experience with trauma indicated I had little ability to cope, much less offer help to others.

Later that morning, after putting Michael on the bus, I lingered at the kitchen table with a cup of coffee. We had recently moved him to Heathwood Hall, a private school with small classes. With my head feeling tight from lack of sleep, I took aspirin to stave off another headache.

The migraines began the day before, when his head teacher his informed me that Michael still refused to turn in homework and was disrupting the class. Added to this, the mother of one of his playmates called, saying, "I'm sorry to tell you this, Gail, but Michael is eating us out of house and home. He went through our weekly stash of cookies and had a bad attitude when I confronted him with it. Maybe he and Edmund should take a break for a while."

I determined that I would speak to Steve that night about a course of action. Finishing the last of the coffee, I glanced down at a stack of disorganized papers, realizing that I hadn't yet looked at Michael's school pictures. Opening the envelope, I noticed signs of depression that I hadn't seen before: lackluster, soulless eyes, frowning brows, and limp, slumped shoulders.

As I glared anxiously at the pictures, I heard a knock at the front door. I was happy to greet Linda Welsford, a close friend. Linda and her husband, Glen, a Presbyterian minister, had ties to an evangelical outreach organization. Showing her Michael's picture, I began voicing my concerns.

Seeing my fragile state, she said, "Gail, I hope you won't be offended, but I'd like to suggest some reading."

"Sure, Linda, what is it?"

Timidly, she said, "Well, it's in the New Testament. The Gospel of John."

4

I deflected it, saying "Thank you, Linda, but I think I've lost all interest in God."

Later that afternoon, I went to the library and began reading John. Passages accusing the Jews of killing Jesus and calling them "children of the devil" confirmed my every suspicion about Christian anti-Semitism. I rushed to the Christian bookstore with the hope that I would come to a different understanding of these dreadful passages.

I found instead Philip Yancey's book *Where is God When it Hurts?* Seeing a brilliant red rose on the cover, I expected a trite treatment of a profound issue. Much to my surprise, Yancey, a scholar, mystic, and philosopher, presented the Christian theology of pain in a clear, nuanced way.[1]

Over time, in grappling with these ideas, a force drew me outside of myself—or perhaps toward my true self—into the life of God. Though our grim situation didn't change, the Christian worldview gave meaning to my pain and allowed me to move forward. I developed intimacy with a God who offers tangible hope, even in an age of Auschwitz. Growing into this new awareness, my emotional terrain evolved from insubstantial and uncertain to settled and firm.

As I sought understanding of life's big questions, God opened my eyes to the innocent suffering at the center of the universe. Anguish that could have destroyed me became a portal into a realm with the only voice capable of stilling it. Coming to understand the sacred meaning of sorrow, in its full array of drama and redemption, enabled me to let go of pessimism and enjoy a life tempered with gratitude.

During Michael's drug years, his counselors who had survived addiction themselves conveyed the most hope. As Michael shared his experience with them, they could stand in his shoes. He, in turn, could identify with their success in recovery.

---

1. Yancey, *Where is God?* then why is it that . . . ? You've heard that question, perhaps asked it yourself. No matter how you complete it, at its root lies the issue of pain. Does God order our suffering? Does he decree an abusive childhood, orchestrate a jet crash, steer a tornado through a community? Or did he simply wind up the world's mainspring and now is watching from a distance? In this Gold Medallion Award-winning book, Philip Yancey reveals a God who is neither capricious nor unconcerned. Using examples from the Bible and from his own experiences, Yancey looks at pain—physical, emotional, and spiritual—and helps us understand why we suffer. *Where is God When it Hurts?* will speak to those for whom life sometimes just doesn't make sense. And it will help equip anyone who wants to reach out to someone in pain but just doesn't know what to say.

I can apply this to my faith journey. In my Jewish walk, a non-observant one, God availed himself to me in personal, intimate ways by sustaining my prayer life. Despite grasping his infinite nature, I discerned limits on his ability to inhabit my actual heartbreak. Jesus, as the God-man, served to bridge this gap. When Jesus entered humanity, he could intuit the substance of my variable savory emotional life, identify with me as both fellow traveler and counselor, and point me toward final victory.

Jesus experienced unspeakable sorrow every time he witnessed a loved one in agony. In my struggle to overcome my addictive enmeshment with Michael, Jesus shouldered the full burden of my grief—that which I couldn't bear and still remain healthy.

Jesus' experience of God-forsakenness on the cross tells me that my spirit can never sink so low that God has not gone deeper still. I conclude in folksy fashion: "Jesus may not take away the pain, but he sure is good company."

Later, in dealing with the terrible mistakes I made as a mother, I became convinced that Christianity affords greater power for forgiveness than Judaism.

I might have ended up a shallow shopaholic had I not come up against an impenetrable wall of pain. My sheltered upbringing kept suffering at a distance, giving me the impression that nothing could ever touch me. I assumed that if I played by the rules and met realistic standards, I could control my destiny. Like many in my immediate circle, I lived life on the surface, content with my lucky status. When in my thirties I was confronted by Michael's problems, all easy assumptions fell away.

Three years after entering the Christian bookstore, I committed my life to Christ in an informal prayer. Living in the same city as my parents, I guarded my privacy for more than fifteen years. I did this out of respect, and because, at the time, I had little confidence in my ability to effectively communicate the depth and richness of what I had come to know.

CHAPTER 2

Early Recollections and
Family Characters

MY ANCESTORS ON BOTH sides came from Russia and Poland during the late-nineteenth and early-twentieth centuries. They held fast to their secular traditions while embracing the opportunities found here in America. Never taking for granted their freedoms and the value of an education, every academic or social achievement validated their progress over the previous generation. Gratitude and pride in accomplishment gave them a healthy identification as Jews and as Americans.

Despite having similar educational and cultural backgrounds, my parents' families of origin had significant emotional differences. Dad's had more traditional values, while Mom's, with a decidedly creative bent, had a propensity toward things whimsical and eccentric.

Dad's siblings, highly intelligent and expansive, had a finely tuned social radar that helped them stay ahead of the game—first, in Estill, South Carolina, and, later, in the capital city of Columbia. My ears always perked up to hear Aunt Evelyn's earthy, guileless brand of gossip. Anyone veering even slightly off the beaten track she deemed a "character." With good-natured curiosity and a trace of thinly guised admiration, she undoubtedly used the designation to refer to someone on Mom's side of the family.

Mom's family moved from Atlanta to Gainesville, Georgia, when Mom was ten. Then a sleepy, rural community, it now thrives as a suburb of Atlanta. The combination of their delightful irreverence and a layer of Southern graciousness afforded them great popularity. Mom, having an unselfconscious pride in her heritage, always started conversations by announcing that she was Jewish.

Not having a synagogue in the vicinity, my grandmother Dora, affectionately called Mudge, fell into the whirl of civic and social activities at the

7

local Presbyterian Church. The youth group elected Mom president, undoubtedly their first Jewish one. This circumstance had as much to do with Mom's genial personality as with the remarkable openness of the church and wider community.

Mom's first cousin, Jack Kurtz, served in the Third Army under General George Patton. Patton and Field Marshal Montgomery had a running debate on which of their armies had the smartest enlisted men. One day, Montgomery challenged Patton to a bet, saying, "George, I'll give you ten dollars if one of your men can get into Oxford."

Patton's men suggested that Jack give it a try. He made his way to Oxford where, as part of an admission's strategy, he sought the favor of his English literature professor. Facing the class, Jack proceeded to recite the entire prologue to *The Canterbury Tales* in Old English. The quirky combination of Old English and his Southern drawl created quite a stir. Jack matriculated to Oxford, and Patton won his ten-dollar bet.

After Jack read the law in Charleston, South Carolina, he met Florence Huxford, a local beauty queen. Florence had attended the Truman inaugural ball with Walter Winchell and was known to have dated the well-known magnate Huntington Hartford. In his column, Winchell wrote, "Miss Huxford will either marry Huntington Hartford or some local boy back home." As it happened, she chose the local boy back home, my uncle Jack. After his two boys were born, Jack went on to create the successful business of Charleston Plywood.

Jack loved nothing more than to recount riotous anecdotes passed down as family lore. His favorite topic centered on Mom's father, Gus, renowned as a practical joker who created a joyful ruckus wherever he went. Once, when asked why he changed his name from Sevelovitz to Meyers, he wryly replied, "I didn't want it to sound too Jewish."

Gus made no secret of the fact that he didn't cotton to Mudge's cooking. Despite her best efforts, the entire household shared Gus's complaint—that is, everyone except their dog, Flossie. Once, at breakfast, Gus said, "Mudge, don't you think we should be careful about letting Flossie get so close to the table? If one of your biscuits fell on her, it'd likely kill her."

Mudge had difficulty keeping a housekeeper; when she finally found Norma, everyone had high hopes. Mudge's job didn't allow for flexibility, so Gus, owner of the local drugstore, always came home to check on things.

One day, he said, "Norma, there's something I haven't told you about Mudge's past. Do you remember that circus that used to be outside of town?"

"Sure, Mr. Gus, I took my kids there when they were young."

He continued, "Well, Mudge used to work there as a lion tamer. Things were getting along just fine until she got attached to a lion cub named Tipsy. She pleaded and pleaded, and I finally agreed that Tipsy could come live with us."

Norma's eyes widened, and she asked, "Where do you keep this here lion, Mr. Gus?"

Gus answered, "Norma, haven't you ever wondered why we keep the downstairs closet locked?

"No, Mr. Gus," she said.

Gus said, "Well, Tipsy lives there. We give her sedatives to calm her, so promise me, Norma, whatever you do, please don't go near that closet without me."

He added, "Follow me, Norma, so I can acquaint you. If Tipsy knows your voice, everything will be just fine."

Norma muttered something under her breath but when Gus turned around, Norma was nowhere to be found. She had hightailed it faster than Gus could even bat an eye. No one in Gainesville ever caught sight of her again.

As the oldest of three girls born to Patricia and Lee Baker, I often wonder what my early years would have looked like under the gaze of God's radical acceptance. So much fallen confidence wasted. Today, as a new creation, I can salvage light where, before, I could find only emptiness. How often I could have relied on these words from the psalmist:

> For thou, O Lord, art my hope,
>
> my trust, O Lord, from my youth.
>
> Upon thee I have leaned from my birth;
>
> thou art he who took me from my mother's womb.
>
> My praise is continually of thee (Ps 71:5–6).

A diffident child with performance anxiety, I feigned sickness in grammar school every time I had to give an oral book report. I savored the time at home with Mom and our longtime housekeeper, Loretta. They attended to my needs with ebullient chatter as they organized the odd and sundry items in my blue-and-white French provincial bedroom. Mom made the delectable, family remedy called "orange and albumen"—orange juice with a thick, sugary meringue topping.

Taking in their chitchat and healing ministrations, I gazed longingly at three impressionistic-style portraits of Kleenex advertising beauties. Coiffed in tones of blonde, brunette, and auburn, they hung on the wall above my dresser—the one we designated as queen for the month was always in a prominent position.

We listened to Mom's favorite music—either Grieg's *Peer Gynt Suite* or Rachmaninoff's *Symphony No. 2*. I relished the order and ritual as well as their cheerful fawning. But most of all, I took comfort from the fact that I had orchestrated a credible ruse, never having to fear giving another oral book report.

I always had a sense that I didn't quite fit in the world. Even from an early age, I felt a level of discomfort in groups. My dreamy, abstracted nature elicited teasing for reasons I could never understand. Later, teachers affirmed that I had a deep imaginative capacity. As personality rolls out when least expected, mine appears funny, despite my best efforts. A friend once complained, "I'm so normal. I need some added zip to my personality. Tell me, how do you do it?"

I responded, "Trust me, I tried being someone else, but it didn't work."

Lacking even slight athletic ability, I dreaded the playground. In the cafeteria at lunchtime, I had to search long and hard for friends to sit with. Though I made above-average grades in math, I had difficulty calculating numbers in my head. When I realized that others didn't count on their fingers, as I did, I developed math phobia.

When I asked Mom the secret to popularity, she said, "Honey, the surefire way to having lots of friends is to always be yourself." If I'd hoped for another gem, I didn't get it.

It would take many years for me to reach the level of self-acceptance Mom so deftly hinted at. It came not from a source within but from one without: When the universe proffered me the gift of Jesus, it afforded me a love so crystalline and pure that every negative conception of myself fell away. Though it came unbidden, often scattershot and diffused, it came nonetheless. Embracing this new order of experience, I gained in the bargain verve, spritely confidence, and an impish sense of humor.

Today, if in God's presence, I can imagine his affirmation: "Gail, this is precisely the way I made you. Why would you ever want to change?" I can only conclude that, unwittingly, my self-esteem has been irrevocably nailed to the cross.

Despite my insecurities, I recall an idyllic childhood. We lived big in Mom's house. With Dad in the background, her values and opinions held sway. With my play reflecting Mom's singular love of fairies, I flit from one activity to another, enveloped in their wonder and enchantment.

The unstinting beauty of this mythological fancy resonated in the deepest part of me. Like a beautiful haunting, it left me with hints of distant lands and sunlit regions where, as Frodo said, in J. R. R. Tolkien's *Lord of the Rings*, "All things sad will become untrue."[1] Though darkness would eclipse this vision for extended periods of my life, its light stood as a beacon holding me to the possibility of things unseen.

Dad died fourteen years ago, Mom seven years later. With the benefit of distance, I now see their qualities in tones of gray rather than as stark black-and-white realities, with even their faults appearing as the underside of virtues perfectly rounded.

As I reflect on them, I'm reminded of George Bernard Shaw's dictum: "Imitation is not the sincerest form of flattery, it's the sincerest form of learning."[2] Though they often stumbled over life's obstacles, their dignity and resilience enabled them to grow stronger in the broken places. I remember them not for their irregular bits and sharp edges but for their graces.

It must have confounded Mom when, early in their courtship, Dad quoted the entirety of Alfred Tennyson's "Crossing the Bar," a poem about death. As for Mom, she could count the many ways she loved Elizabeth Barrett Browning. If she saw the world through rose-colored glasses, Dad's vision bore hardly a tint. While beauty stirred Mom to raptures, Dad's humdrum, prosaic nature knew no such longings. From her, I gained a picture of an ideal world, no rose garden perhaps, but an enchanted landscape full of mystery and romance. Dad exemplified practical no-nonsense standards and the value of carrying out simple kindnesses behind the scenes with little fanfare.

Mom's sentiments tilted toward the poetic and ethereal. She documented her wholehearted striving to go beneath the surface of things in countless journals. In her wallet, she carried a quote attributed to Anaïs Nin: "And

1. Tolkien, *Return of King*.
2. Kirov, *George Bernard*, 26.

the day came when the risk to remain tight in a bud was more painful than the risk it took to blossom."[3] Having transcendent moments that the French call *jouissants*, she often regaled us with her latest enthusiasm—bird watching, kaleidoscopes, tea parties, or her new best friend.

As an empath—one who psychically tunes in with the emotions of others—Mom had an artless, unaffected love for people. Because she never criticized or gossiped, as a teenager I found her trusting and naïve to a fault. Later, I realized that she saw precisely what others revealed—nothing more and nothing less. Because of her high ideals, many put their best foot forward around her, causing her to see a narrower spectrum of traits than most of us see.

Unfortunately, Mom's way of expressing emotions caused a level of chaos and consternation. She often said the opposite of what she meant. After stating a lofty observation or opinion, more times than not she backtracked to give a more reasoned authentic response. Because her messages lacked clarity and resolve, I grew up doubting my instincts and perceptions.

Mom's effortless compassion seemed congenitally bound to her bloodstream. For years, I defined myself in opposition to her, throwing the baby out with the bathwater. As I grew older and came to admire in others the very qualities that I disparaged in her, my defenses began to crumble. Today, I consider it the ultimate compliment if someone compares me to her.

Now, I see that Mom's example prepared me to recognize the mercy shown by Jesus. Though in her it seemed forced—overblown and dramatic—from Jesus, it must have emanated naturally.

The effect of multiple tragedies in Dad's grandparents' lives must have filtered down to shape his outlook. Even as a child, I could sense in him a formless void. Later, recognizing it as dour, stoical secularism, I determined not to let it map my future. I held my head upright, hoping for a whiff of different air.

Because Dad was not given to reflection or heart-to-heart conversation, I found his nature baffling. Despite winning awards for oratory, he had difficulty showing his private emotions, something that weighed on our family. This lack of expression, either consciously chosen or from scant self-knowledge, made him appear imprisoned inside himself. I needed a crystal ball to know what he thought of my capabilities. Because I sensed impatience in him, what he didn't say loomed more terrifying in my imagination than what little he did say.

3. Nin, *Quotable Anais Nin*, 37.

During Dad's developmental years, he supervised his younger brother, Edward, who suffered speech and hearing loss as a young child. They communicated through sign language and writing. Because of their bond, an aura of silence may have permeated Dad's personality. After my Grandmother Esther's funeral, Edward joined us for lunch at my parents' house. As the afternoon progressed, I wrote, "Edward, why don't you visit with Dad in the library?"

Shaking his head, he penned, "I don't want to disturb him. Lee is a man of few words."

Dad and his cousin Dave managed a successful commercial real-estate company. They both enjoyed respect from business associates throughout the city. At contentious business meetings, Dad always brought about consensus through his use of sparse, judiciously chosen words. His gentle demeanor caused an associate to remark, "When Lee Baker talks, everyone listens."

Over the years, I grew to understand that what Dad couldn't—or didn't—verbalize, he expressed through actions. When the two of us began taking emotional risks, we were able to communicate on a deeper level. I consider it one of the great blessings of my life that we finally developed an intimate, unshakable bond.

A product of the Depression, Dad wanted to succeed so that he could provide an education for his girls. A humorous story told by our good friend Reese Williams illustrates Dad's attitude toward money. Instead of upgrading his Cadillac every few years, he bought used parts for repairs. Once, the parts salesman asked, "Lee, why don't you just buy another Cadillac? You can certainly afford it."

In classic deadpan, he answered, "Well, the money I could use for a new Cadillac could go towards a Kmart mortgage. Hopefully, that money, in five years, would accrue to ten thousand dollars and, in another five years, to twenty. Now, I just have to say, I just can't afford a Cadillac that expensive."

I've heard it said, "Every marriage is a foreign country." Whatever the nature of the mysterious alchemy holding their parallel universes together, it appeared to work for my parents rather than against them. They often used humor to accommodate their differences. Once, at the International House of Pancakes, a cheerful waitress approached our table. Mom smiled at her, saying, "My, you have such beautiful skin. What's your name, sweetheart?"

"Oh, thank you. My name is Valerie."

After Mom and I ordered, Dad, without looking up, said, "I'll have two eggs, sunny side up, with apple pancakes."

After Valerie left, Mom said, "Lee, you were downright rude to that waitress."

He impishly replied, "Honey, I don't have to be so nice. You're nice enough for two of us."

Mom enjoyed exploring the woods near her house at any time of day and in any type of weather. The first day of spring was cause for her to celebrate and discover. As she readied for a trek with Michael, she turned to Dad, asking, "Honey, why don't you join us?"

He responded, "No, thanks, honey, I've seen it all before."

As their divergence played out, I had difficulty integrating the conflicting sides of my nature. My left and right brain were at odds with one another: one side reflected Mom and the other, Dad. This caused my difficulty in making decisions. Like Mom, I had a delayed reaction, not knowing exactly what I thought about a matter.

Observing them helped me to detect the vast space within the human heart that remains inscrutable, elusive, and variable. I learned to hold opposite views in tension and gained an appreciation for moderation, mystery, and paradox. In my thirties, for example, while struggling to negotiate faith and identity, I assumed the label, "a congregation of one."

CHAPTER 3

All Things Jewish

IF OUR EARLIEST IMPRESSIONS form and inform how we categorize the world, the phrase "culture wars" defined mine. In our middle-to-upper-class area, I divided people into two groups: Christian country-club Republicans and Jewish liberal Democrats. In this set up, our community stood on the outside.

Our values resembled those of Jewish families who moved to the suburbs after World War II. We erected synagogues at the same pace that our Christian neighbors built churches. Like many first-generation Jews, Dad went to synagogue not to worship but to congregate with other Jews. The year he assumed the presidency of our Conservative Beth Shalom Synagogue, he informed me that he didn't believe in God.

We attended services once a year, on the High Holidays. After a group Bat Mitzvah, I continued going to Sunday school, which, except for Dr. Gerald Breger's philosophical lectures, I found tedious and boring. Today, I still struggle with the Hebrew liturgy and have little knowledge of Jewish customs and rituals. Curiously, Mom always taught us to say Jewish person rather than Jew. Presumably, Jew had a negative connotation. When I asked her about it, she simply said, "It just sounds nicer." I find it telling that the words *Jew* and *Jesus*, both shot through with divine intension, have become epithets.

I recall utter disillusionment when I learned that one of my favorite uncles changed his last name from Levinson to Lawrence to avoid anti-Semitism in the air force. Years later, when he heard his teenage boys voicing anti-Semitic slurs, he informed them about their heritage.

Even today, I bristle in thinking about my uncle's decision. Once, chiding me for self-righteousness, Steve said, "Gail, you have no right to talk. After all, you've left the fold entirely."

Countering it, I said, "Honey, I didn't leave for convenience sake. I left out of conviction. You wouldn't think highly of a fan who left his favorite sports team just because they were going through a losing streak."

My first brush with anti-Semitism occurred in grammar school, when some in our neighborhood wanted to exclude us from a carpool. Patsy Malanuk's mother, Nita Craig, heard about the plan and squelched it immediately.

In high school, inured to the ever-present efforts to proselytize, I had many non-Jewish friends. Because of my assimilation, I had greater aware-ness of anti-Semitism than my Jewish friends who stayed in their narrow circle. Reflecting the social ethic of teenagers and their instinct for following the herd, I had a hard time accepting my difference. I felt more distress over subtle social slights than anti-Semitism's more blatant forms.

When I was in middle school, our family received vicious anti-Semitic telephone calls. The comments ranged from "Christ killer" and "filthy kike" to "nigger lover." We involved the FBI, who traced the calls to several of my so-called friends at school. Because of their popularity, word spread rapidly. The expression on the face of my best gentile friend implied that our family had committed an egregious offense by calling them to account.

Since that time, I have learned that the FBI was mistaken about the identity of the callers. I regret that gossip and innuendo have caused harm to those unjustly accused.

Later, in coming to embrace a category of "good different," I cultivated an independent streak and the outlook of an outsider, helping me to develop a strong sense of character and a refined sense of justice. Today, in an alter-nate current and with different markers on the shoreline, I still swim against the tide. I experience knotting tension every time I encounter Christian anti-Semitism or rigid cultural stereotypes about faith and identity.

Dad once chided, "If you scratch below the surface of any gentile, you'll find deep pockets of anti-Semitism." Mom and Dad had strong working relationships with even those Christians who lived in neighborhoods that had restrictions on Jews—one of whom unabashedly asked Dad, "Can't you understand why we just want to keep our neighborhoods Christian?"

My parents' understanding of Jewish values motivated them to give back to Columbia's larger civic and cultural community. Because of their relentless efforts on behalf of such groups as the Salvation Army, the Co-lumbia Museum of Art, the Girl Scouts, and the Columbia Music Festival Association, they received numerous accolades and awards. Mom especially loved her time with Howard McLean and Philip Whitehead on the interfaith Christian Action Council.

In high school, I balked when my parents objected to my serious relationship with a non-Jewish boy. Later, as president of his Kappa Alpha fraternity, he invited me to their Old South weekend at Wofford College. Dad said, "I can't relate to Southern values as such. Your date's family could have owned slaves while ours were fighting the czars in Russia. Don't forget who you are."

My parents, card-carrying members of the American Civil Liberties Union, resisted the placement of Christian symbols on public property. It's interesting that, today, the Orthodox group Chabad has a giant menorah on the grounds of the South Carolina State House. At one time, it stood near the controversial Confederate flag, which was removed in 2015 after the Charleston church massacres.

We celebrated Hanukkah and Passover as tributes to cultural freedom without any emphasis on the miraculous. Hanukkah, a minor festival, gets played out in America as a major one because of its occurrence in the Christmas season. Mom always carved a large Jewish star out of Styrofoam and placed it on a bed of angel hair, surrounded by blue-and-white lights. My sisters, Janna and Laurie, and I helped her loop silver chains from the chandelier and valance.

One year, the last night of Hanukkah fell on Christmas Eve. After opening our gifts, we readied for bed, when Laurie and I implored Mom to wake us up at 2:00 a.m.

"Why in the world would you want to get up then?" she asked.

I said, "We want to watch Santa come to the Otts' house." The Otts were the only Christian family on Wyndham Road, our small Jewish cul-de-sac.

Reluctantly, Mom said, "Oh, I guess I'll wake you."

Laurie and I shared a room with two beds placed at right angles to an oversized toy bin. Above, wide horizontal windows let in a panoramic view of the entire neighborhood. When Mom came in to wake us, we opened the blinds, raised ourselves to our knees and peered outside for what felt like hours. Having no amount of jealousy, we felt only keen expectation and unbridled joy at the prospect of experiencing Christmas through Mary Ott's eyes. As sleep overtook us, we determined to alter next year's vigil, so that we could catch Santa in the act.

Passover, my favorite holiday, commemorates the end of Israelite bondage and symbolizes mankind's hope for an end to discrimination and prejudice. On the first night, our family always hosted a ceremonial meal called a Seder.

The longing and joy of nostalgia take me back to a time of carefree abandon during school break. Sitting on our front lawn, I awaited the arrival of relatives—the cast of characters introduced earlier. I delighted in signs of incipient spring—the newly formed forsythia blossoms and crocuses bursting from the loamy soil. I took in the rich savory aroma of Mom's chicken soup that emanated from the kitchen window. As a breeze tussled my hair, I selected the best specimens from an array of flowers to fashion a clover necklace. The previous year, Mudge had taught me how to carefully slit and entwine their delicate stems to avoid breaking them.

Our relatives' incongruous mix of personalities made great fodder for entertainment. Mudge's love of spectacle and her instinct for the theatrical meant that Laurie, Janna, and I could take bets on the many ways she could embarrass Dad with her antics. On this night, she plopped down on the floor to display her calisthenics and told her latest off-color joke. Though its meaning was lost on me at the time, Aunt Evelyn later informed me it could have made a seasoned sailor blush.

Though Dad adored Mudge, I heard him whisper to Mom, "Sometimes she reminds me of an Eastern European circus performer."

At another interval, Mudge, looking at Dad, asked, "Lee, when the time comes, will you help with my funeral expenses?"

Dad said, "Mudge, I'll be glad to bury you."

Passover as a teenager took on a different timbre. I always helped Mom set a table to include politicos from liberal interest groups. (We never met one we didn't like.) Our table—modern, lacquered, and walnut—differed from the antique ones belonging to my gentile friends. Dad could never understand why anyone would want to buy what he called "used furniture."

Increasingly, I had noticed that our Seders lacked sacred content and context. As head of the household, Dad led the service using a book called a Haggadah. We often joked about passing over Passover because we used the abbreviated version. After recounting the ancient biblical story, Dad said, "Well, I hate to be a party-pooper, but I just can't believe that the exodus actually happened. I've been reading *Man and His Gods*, by Homer Smith, and *Biblical Archeology Review*. They both cast doubt."

Though *Biblical Archeology Review* proves reliable on this score,[1] *Man and His Gods* reflects a typical Enlightenment approach in which social

1. Hoffmeier, "Out of Egypt."

scientists, psychologists, and anthropologists reduce, prod, and analyze the entire religious experience.[2]

Mom interjected, saying, "Whether it's historical or not, doesn't it say something about God's protection of his people?" Her conversations were an unpredictable brio, drawing from Shirley McLaine's New Age aphorisms or serious insights from the Great Books curriculum. She had immersed herself in this study under Mortimer Adler at the University of Chicago.

Between the gefilte fish and the chicken soup, my cousin, Susan, asked, "Did you hear that David Williams got into Harvard? He spent last summer interning at the ACLU. His dad actually marched with civil rights leaders in Alabama."

Knowing of this gentile family, I smiled and wryly asked, "Are you sure he's not Jewish?"

Mom laughed and said, "Well, if he's not, he should be."

Aunt Evelyn, the consummate storyteller, said, "Boy, do I have a tale for you. We all know how much Senator Rubin loves to pontificate on Democratic Party politics and issues related to Israel. Last week, he overheard a conversation between his young granddaughter, Rosie, and Jackie, her gentile girlfriend. Jackie asked, 'Rosie, how do you get to be Jewish?' Without missing a beat, Rosie said, 'You need to be voted in, of course.'"

Everyone laughed and applauded Rosie's cleverness. Only later did I see the subtle half-truth that in many quarters, Judaism gets played out as a secular political response. In his article, "The Decline and Rise of Secular Judaism," Edwin Shapiro pointed out the many ways in which Jews express their identity other than religion: fundraising for Israel, fighting anti-Semitism, and attending book or film festivals. He stated that many who engage only in these activities run the risk of spiritual emptiness.[3]

Albert Einstein, a skeptic who retained his Jewish identity, saw no inconsistency when he considered accepting the post as president of the Medical College of Yeshiva, a leading American Orthodox institution.[4] That current college courses on Judaism focus on sociology and history, rather than on religion, and that gentiles serve on the boards of Reform synagogues (not a bad thing itself) prove that religion is not the only tie that binds Jews together.

2. Smith, *Man and His Gods.*
3. Shapiro, "Decline and Rise."
4. "Offering Presidency."

Increasingly, many favor the option of non-religious cultural conversion, one that allows gentiles to identify and affiliate with the Jewish people. They reason that an agnostic gentile should not have to go through a rabbi to become an agnostic Jew.

Seeing the importance of continuity in the face of anti-Semitism, our family stressed the centrality of Jewish roots from the historical and national to the familial and individual. Though having great empathy for those on the margins of society, Mom and Dad had little awareness that feeding the poor and healing the sick were ancient biblical values. Unknowingly, they stood on the shoulders of the prophetic giants who came before them.

Judaism attempts a balance between the opposing ideals of the universal and particular. For example, though Israel has a unique covenant with God, the rabbis emphasize that the righteous of all the nations will merit a place in the world to come. During my developmental years, Mom and Dad tilted toward the universal with broad-based humanitarian values trumping the narrow focus on Israel. I grew up with buzzwords such as tolerant, humanistic, progressive, and egalitarian—all based on the assumption that mankind is essentially good—and that the right utopian system can cure all of society's ills. Somewhere in this potpourri of values and opinions, I concluded that the word *liberal* inevitably meant *loving*.

Later, focusing on the needs of worldwide Jewry, Mom and Dad developed a strong idealist bond with early Zionism. (Zionism is the national movement that supports the re-establishment of a Jewish homeland in Israel.)

In the period leading up to 1967, Egyptian forces mobilized along the Sinai Peninsula. Israel launched pre-emptive air strikes in which they defeated Egypt, Jordan, and Syria. It occupied the Sinai Peninsula, the Gaza Strip, the West Bank, East Jerusalem, and the Golan Heights.

The Six-Day War broke out during my senior year in high school. The media's constant focus on Israel's military prowess caused it to be the topic of conversation in many of my classes. I could hardly wait for the Israeli fundraiser Mom and Dad planned to host at our house.

Arriving home from school, that day, I saw that Loretta had already prepared the appetizers and vacuumed the house. As Mom got out her best wine glasses, Dad peppered her with questions about the agenda. "Do you think Albert should speak first?" As head of Columbia's Jewish Federation, Albert planned local fundraisers and educational events.

"No," she said. "Definitely not. Adam should go first because of his recent trip to Israel. His enthusiasm will get the ball rolling. After that, Albert can speak about the financial needs.

Mom said, "Lee, I've never seen you like this before. You've always been involved, but this is beyond the pale. Where's it all coming from?"

Dad said, "I'm not sure. I just know that I can't take my identity for granted any longer. If Jews don't help other Jews, no one else will. Just look at the Holocaust."

The guests arrived, about fifty men in all, first filling the living room, then the screened-in porch. Most of them had serious faces, almost on the verge of tears. After Dad welcomed everyone, he called on Adam to speak.

Adam gave some preliminary remarks about his trip, and then turned to Mom. "Pat, I was so proud to see your name prominently displayed at Hadassah Hospital. Thank you so much for your tireless efforts on behalf of this very worthy cause."

For years, Mom had raised money for Hadassah, a women's Zionist organization that funds a hospital in Jerusalem. Here, Jewish and Arab doctors work in harmony on cutting-edge worldwide research. In 2002, because of its equal treatment of ethnic and religious minorities, Hadassah Hospital was nominated for the Nobel Peace Prize.[5]

Adam continued, saying, "Honestly, our trip changed me. I've never felt such pride in my identity. Just think of it—we Jews have spawned the entire moral fabric of Western civilization. It's time to put our identity on the line. Israel will perish if we don't ante up."

Chiming in, Dad said, "As most of you know, I'm not a religious man, but I agree with Adam. The Jewish word for charity is *tzedakah*. Today, charity is not a subjective choice. It's a holy obligation. Because a secure Israel can deter worldwide anti-Semitism, we should give for selfish reasons."

Albert gave an emotional pitch detailing Israel's financial needs before passing out the pledge cards. The electric atmosphere rose to a crescendo as each man got up to announce his commitment. I watched in amazement as the group raised more than one hundred thousand dollars that night.

I experienced newfound pride as well as an appreciation for the role Jews have played throughout history. I witnessed my parents' love for the Jewish people. Over the years, they showed me how marriage partners can work harmoniously to achieve shared goals.

5. "Learning Why Hadassah Hospital."

Despite the continued legitimacy of such consciousness-raising sessions, as my spirituality evolved I experienced a void. The fervor and zeal expressed over nationhood and continuity began to resemble an idol, a substitute for God.

In his book *A Certain People: American Jews and Their Lives Today*, Charles Silberman noted that the 1967 war changed the way most Jews felt about themselves. Allegiance to Israel became the center of communal life and the primary means for Jews to affirm their identity. As a result, spirituality took the backseat.[6]

The 2013 Pew Research Survey, "A Portrait of Jewish Americans," documented responses to the question, "What is Essential to Being Jewish?" 73 percent of respondents listed the Holocaust as the primary requisite of Jewish identity, as opposed to, for example, "Leading an Ethical and Moral Life" (69 percent), "Caring about Israel" (43 percent), and "Observing Jewish law" (19 percent).[7]

Given my intense focus on the Holocaust, I was confounded by the position taken by eminent Jewish scholar Joseph Neusner in the *Journal of Religion*. Only someone as widely published could have expressed the provocative view that Jews take Holocaust remembrance and their focus on survival to an unhealthy extreme. He wrote that this obsession obscured Judaism's inherent spirituality.[8]

6. Silberman, *A Certain People*, 199.
7. "A Portrait."
8. Neusner, "Implications of Holocaust."

CHAPTER 4

Notes of Discord

AN EARLY ONSET TO puberty while still a preteen caused me to feel my body had somehow betrayed me. In the amorphous space between childhood and independence to come, adulthood both appealed to me and repelled me. Stalling for time, perhaps symbolically, I danced for hours to the music from the Broadway musical *Peter Pan* on our wrap-around porch.

The bathroom I shared with Janna and Laurie had pink-floral wallpaper and a mirror placed at right angles above two vanities. Even at eleven, I had the weekly ritual of Mom washing my hair in the bathtub. I no longer needed her help but didn't know how to tell her.

When I emerged dripping wet, she enveloped me in a soft, almond-scented Turkish wrap. We sang a silly little ditty, "Ho, hum, diddly, dee, now I see, now I see," as she towel-dried my hair. Making up outrageous nonsense words to complete the stanzas, we erupted in laughter. I loved the almond residue that lingered on my body and seeped into the bed linens overnight. Even today, the aroma brings to mind the simplicity of my childhood affection for Mom.

One night, my hair completely dry, Mom continued singing alone. As her voice trailed off, she giggled nervously and appeared self-conscious.

I asked, "What is it, Mom? You remind me of Mr. Twiggly." Mr. Twiggly was a favorite cartoon character, who never let on his true feelings.

"Time is just moving so fast," she said tenderly. Soon you won't need my help with your hair."

Confused at first, I blurted out, "You're right. Next week I'll do it by myself."

I saw Mom's overprotection as an odd quirk—nothing to raise red flags. As I grew, however, I began noticing unpleasant realities in our family culture. Janna, Laurie, and I weren't allowed to show even a hint of backbiting, competition, or disagreement—normal things expected of girls three years apart. Courteous to the point of parody, we mimicked characters on shows such as *Pollyanna* or *Father Knows Best*. Not being able to voice constructive criticism about such innocuous things as clothes or hairstyles meant I lacked the easy confidence that grows organically from an honest home base. Once, when I innocently suggested that Janna part her hair differently, Mom excoriated me for hurting Janna's feelings. As this dance of mock harmony played out, I ended up the last one standing after Mom cast me as the mean one in the family.

During these years, I savored long summer evenings playing kickball with my younger friends in the neighborhood. As the sun and whisper of enchanted birdsong began to wane, hordes of fireflies invaded our space. When they darted luminously in every direction, we scattered to find jars for capturing them.

One night, no longer sensing the thrill, I came in early. Resting in bed, I glanced up at the Hollywood-style mirror standing on my dresser and saw that in lieu of the baby fat which once defined my face I now had delicately sculpted features. Before this night, I had never thought of myself as particularly pretty. Whatever good looks I came to possess, I see that they worked both for and against me. I've used it as a tool for power, a bulwark against my insecurities and a hollow boost to my self-esteem.

At fourteen, I still shared the same bathroom with Janna and Laurie, but with a privacy shade in the window. Mom once came in unannounced when I emerged from the shower. As I reached for the towel, she glanced in my direction. I wish she'd said something like, "You're developing into such a beautiful young woman, Gail. I'm so happy for you." Instead, her expression showed only discomfort, if not downright fear.

Though the memory of this episode remains disquieting, it gave me a chance to move down a path of full-fledged disengagement. I sensed Mom and I had an unspoken agreement that required it. Our bond had become inscrutable, both promissory and provoking. One side of Mom represented romance and light; the other side, power and control. I feared her tentacle-like grasp would stymie all authenticity as I moved into adulthood. The magical spell that my childhood conjured required a visceral lancing.

Playing at our divergence, Mom and I had one small dilemma: Neither of us could foresee how the breach would play out. As it happened, the glow from our halcyon days would cast a shadow that would confound us for years.

If my separation from Mom created a void requiring a divine connection, a certain reverie about God produced the opposite effect. One night, on the edge of sleep, I began to think deeply about the nature of infinity and time. Agitated and confused, I fell into a deep sleep. In my dream, I dared to ask God for solace and understanding. Instead of giving me repose, he saw fit to place me on a narrow, moss-covered precipice high above a basin of water.

Abandoned and in abject despair, I tried to maintain my equilibrium when suddenly I lost my foothold. My soul gave way as I plunged headlong through space. With the cold waters closing around me, I lost all hope of a benevolent God.

I awoke to a sense of being untethered from the universe, alienated from every fond and familiar attachment. The vivid memory of this God forsakenness caused me to fear sleep for weeks. Its impact hovered over me during the next phase of my life, weaving its way into my psyche and keeping every spiritual inclination at bay. Like Maurice Bendix, in Graham Greene's novel *The End of the Affair*, I disliked the very God I refused to believe in.[1]

1. Greene, *End of Affair*, 164.

CHAPTER 5

Adolescent Standoff

INCREASINGLY, I WANTED TO mimic the breezy, shoot-from-the-hip persona of my peers rather than Mom's goody-two-shoes reserve. My adolescent task called for integrating these two ways of being in the world. Though known for my successes in the ruthless competition of high school politics, dating, social clubs, and beauty contests, I felt submerged in a floodtide of loneliness. When calling a friend, for example, I heard the person answering the phone say, "Gail Baker's on the phone." I wanted to be known as just Gail—familiar and one of the girls.

My accomplishments on the outside gave no clue to the devastation I was wreaking on the home front. For years, Mom and I engaged in a furious test of wills. Afraid I would grow up too fast, she wouldn't allow me to mark normal milestones such as using lipstick, wearing pantyhose, or shaving my legs. She insisted that I wear my Girl Scout uniform to school on the day of our meetings. To get around her excessive control, I resorted to lying and subterfuge.

When I especially wanted to get under her skin, I muttered a prejudicial epithet in Loretta's company. My behavior didn't bode well for my relationship with Loretta or Mom's liberal reputation with Loretta's African American friends.

On one occasion, when she wouldn't allow me to attend my high school sorority dance, I yelled, "How could you be so cruel? Everyone I know is going!"

She shouted her favorite admonition, "If you do these things now, you won't have anything to look forward to."

In a piercing register that frightened even me, I growled, "I hate you, and I wish you were dead. You treat me like a two-year-old and you're a horrible mother." My goal was to eviscerate her. She held her role as mother as something sacrosanct never to be tampered with.

"I hate you, too, right now," she shrieked. By now, the entire neighborhood could hear us.

Our coterie of friends, practically like family, entered one another's houses unannounced. If, while visiting, one of them sensed a fight brewing in ours, they left and proceeded to take bets on which one of us would throw the first punch. Within earshot on this particular day, better judgment told them to steer clear of the ruckus.

After hearing my slight on her mothering, Mom slapped me so hard that I fell onto the metal desk. After steadying myself, I grabbed her head and began yanking it back and forth. When she pried me loose, I fell hard to the floor. The excruciating pain in my elbow told me that I had hit the sharp metal edge of the bed frame.

I wailed, "See what you made me do! I can't wait to tell people how abusive you are."

I mustered every ounce of strength for a final act of defiance. Using my good arm, I grabbed her torso, propelled my leg forward, and kicked her clear across the room. She went flying.

Dad, who always bolted at the slightest hint of provocation, cowered in a back room away from it all. Janna and Laurie, looking for cover, hid under the bed with our precious mutt, Licorice. Licorice, with his radar for predicting trouble, always managed to escape before things got out of hand.

Because Mom and I eventually developed such a close relationship, I have difficulty imagining these rampages. Today, I see the benefit of these roller-coaster years. That jealousy, wounds, and insults can cohere with love and forgiveness prepared me for the notion of faith as struggle. Later, in wrangling with God, I could express anger and doubt without fear of rejection.

Many years later, putting together some critical dates, I understood what Mom meant by "growing up too fast." She would have had me make any mistake other than the one she herself made many years ago—that of getting pregnant before marriage. When she came to Columbia, in 1949, this catastrophe made it hard for her to face Dad's family and build new relationships in the Jewish community.

I surmise that we often get the thing we fear most in life because we inadvertently make it happen. Anxiety over a problem can lead to such over-reaction that the opposite can occur. Because of Dad's extreme aversion to any emotional display, Mom created a fairy-tale façade. Afraid that I would get pregnant, she ruled with an iron hand. She should have considered it a blessing that I never even fathomed or got close to getting pregnant before marriage.

Mom's Journal:

A few years of Gail's teenage years were confrontational, to say the least. We clashed head on with verbal as well as physical warfare. Gail was stubbornly fighting for her freedom and independence (thank God for her assertive will to confront me). I was stubbornly refusing it, totally unwise and insensitive to her needs. I should have understood this watershed phase of her life, her need to disconnect, her hormones, and her emotional seesaws. It was my first time parenting an adolescent. Rather than understanding and showing compassion, I continued to battle, at the same time making her the bad guy, a title undeserved. Rather than dealing with these years differently, I continued to play the victim. I should have known better or sought help. On many occasions, I thought of counseling, but found the resources unavailable and infrequently used. Those stormy moments frightened everyone and dismantled our home. We weathered those years, and today Gail and I value each other in a wondrous bond of intimacy, love and laughter. Her spirituality, her wisdom, and her boundless love stretched my heart, making her my anchor and my friend.

CHAPTER 6

Leaving Home

DAD ALWAYS CAME HOME for his big meal in the middle of the day. Because I finished classes early during my senior year, we often sat together at the kitchen table. One day, trying to engage him, I asked, "Dad, what's going on at work?"

"Oh, the usual."

As he perused the newspaper, I asked, "What's new in politics?"

"Oh, not much," he answered.

Knowing that he chaired the Salvation Army's capital campaign, I asked, "How are things going at the Army?"

"We haven't started soliciting, yet," he answered.

When Mom came into the kitchen, her body language signaled thinly veiled tension. With her eyes shifting nervously, she said, "I don't want to interrupt. I hope you two are having a heart-to-heart."

"What?" I asked, wrinkling my brow and laughing at the prospect.

With my single-minded focus on getting away and going to college, I ignored her comment. Revisiting it later, I saw it as an example of her crazy-making behavior. Despite what she said, she didn't want us to bond at all.

I attended the University of North Carolina at Greensboro for two years before transferring to George Washington University in Washington, DC. I graduated in 1971 with a BA in education and psychology.

After living in the parochial South, I found the cosmopolitan atmosphere of GWU exhilarating and liberating. The decisions I made reflected this culture shock. In North Carolina, they revolved around such trivialities as whether to wear Papagallo shoes and pearls. At GWU, they centered on whether to march in the demonstration against the Vietnam War, whether to date an Arab man, or whether to experiment with marijuana—all of which I did in that order.

When Dad expressed his shock to learn that I was dating someone named Mohammad, he asked, "Mohammad who?"

I snipped, "What do you think, Dad? Mohammad Stein." He didn't buy it.

I pranced into those years a shallow egotistical person with little sensitivity to those around me. My excessive rumination over each problem or insecurity caused me to have tunnel vision. I wanted any concern other than the one at hand—which consisted of minor irritations such as being cut from the final round for homecoming queen or not getting attention from a boy that I liked.

The heady collegiate humor at GWU reflected an irony and cool I was sure I lacked. My every insecurity fed on the flair and sophistication of rapid-fire repartee. It emanated from classroom windows and suffocated me like overgrown ivy. Wanting to prove myself, I sought to dispel the impression my Southern accent may have given.

I helped organize a student government symposium in which columnist Art Buchwald participated. I invited Sol Lavisky, a close family friend, to speak at an event attended by hundreds of student radicals. Uncle Sol worked for the Washington branch of Humro, a human-resource firm thought to be part of the military-industrial complex. Facing jeers from the audience, this eloquent Southern gentleman countered with grace, intelligence, and aplomb. At the end of what came to resemble a question-and-answer session, the audience cheered and gave him a standing ovation.

At the time, GWU had problems with student unrest. Mom and Dad, watching news reports on the government's crackdown, feared I lived in a police state. I could only give them the slim assurance that six armed guards stood on every street corner.

On May 3, 1970, I took part in a large-scale demonstration against the Vietnam War. Hoping to shut down the government for a day, demonstrators may have played a key role in damaging Nixon's career. Protesters used jury-rigged barricades, cars, and bodies to block twenty-one key bridges and circles. They came in waves, one group sitting at a target until arrested, when another replaced them. The government placed twelve thousand troops at strategic points to sweep, arrest, and disperse fifteen thousand participants.

The center of the activity took place near the campus in a section of DC called Foggy Bottom. I participated as an unofficial observer, hoping for a story I could someday tell my children. I also wanted to impress a group of friends who had more political savvy.

On a balmy 70-degree morning, I met Bob Rosenfeld in front of my dorm on F Street. Looking across the street at the famous F Street Club, I saw pink and red camellias ready to burst open. Above to our right, a squadron of helicopters patrolled the Washington Monument area. As we walked north on 19th Street, choppers lobbed tear gas and policemen chased protestors running wildly through the streets. At the intersection of 19th and Pennsylvania, officers with lowered helmets faced off with protesters. One, using a large club, attacked a woman in front of us. When a brave bystander attempted to take her photograph, another officer confiscated his camera.

We saw similar skirmishes as we walked up Pennsylvania Avenue. At Washington Square, official protesters communicated with their cohorts on walkie-talkies. Suddenly, out of nowhere, a mounted policeman shot tear gas in my direction. I felt a stinging, burning sensation in my eyes, nose, and mouth. My vision became blurry, and I began coughing and choking. When its effect subsided, I scanned up and down several blocks to find Bob. He was nowhere in sight.

Finally, as I walked up New Hampshire Avenue toward DuPont Circle, I saw a scene that I would revisit again and again as an antidote to an otherwise grueling day: costumed flute players frolicked with carefree abandon around a statue of Gandhi.

Moving toward Connecticut Avenue, I glimpsed the condo belonging to my cousin Jeff Schreiber. Expecting a tumultuous day, Jeff had graciously offered his place as a safe-haven. I arrived around 2:00 p.m., grateful for the reprieve and happy to see Jeff's friendly face. After recounting the day's exhausting events, I took a shower and slept for several hours. Later, I learned that Bob had survived two rounds of tear gas before arriving at his apartment.

I met Steve during my senior year. The first time I saw him, he swaggered towards me in tight-fitting jeans and a denim work shirt. He was darkly handsome, and his masculinity seeped from every pore. After Bob Rosenfeld introduced us, we immediately started dating. I was smitten by his intelligence, urbane wit, and feisty Northern manner. He hails from Greek Orthodox Yankee stock, for whom Zorba-esque exuberance and over-the-top bossiness connote powerful expressions of love. Beneath his take-charge manner and cocky assurance lies a core of unselfish, adoring affection—open, vulnerable, and authentic. I fell, no hesitation.

On our first date, I laughed to myself as he compulsively lined up an assortment of coasters on my coffee table. (I have a hard time finding socks that match.) Our union must have bewildered our friends—Steve, the epitome of common sense, and me, without a practical bone in my body. It would take a Shakespeare, or perhaps God himself, to divine how we've managed intimacy for more than forty-five years.

While Steve was bred on the satire of Mad Magazine, I grew up taking myself so seriously I missed much of life's humor. In our household today, we entertain by playing off one another. I seem to strike his funny bone every time I wax poetic or express some dramatic conviction. All I need do is glance in his direction and see his sardonic smile, and we both burst out laughing.

His witty good-hearted sarcasm gives us an edgy chemistry. Confronted with some of my quirks, Steve often calls me a hoot, a riot, or a trip. My diagnosis of attention deficiency disorder prompted him to say, "You don't have ADD, you just have L-A-Z-Y." He deflects his frustration over this condition with statements like, "Well, I guess Striker [our cat] forgot to lock the back door today," or "I see Striker forgot to turn off the stove." Recently, before leaving for a sailboat race to Cuba, he said, "Please don't pray for me. Take me off your hit list because everyone you pray for dies." Once, when I asked him whether our marriage had improved him, he said, "Well, I've certainly gained a lot more tolerance, and I no longer fear death."

When being fodder for his revelry gets overbearing, I have only to focus on his many acts of devotion. One night, I had left for the airport to catch a flight when Steve noticed that I'd forgotten my computer. Knowing that I couldn't survive without it, he jumped in his car, buck-naked, and flagged me down at the first exit.

Because Steve pushes himself in social situations, many express their shock to learn that he is essentially very shy. As for myself, I have become the very type of person who intimidated me as a child. Our inner radars complement one another's weaknesses, confirming the paradoxical truth of the French, "Vive la différence."

CHAPTER 7

Interfaith Soul Talk

STEVE WORKED AT NASA for several years while I taught first grade in Alexandria, Virginia. Later, we moved to Columbia, where I obtained an MA in special education, and Steve began law school. We married in 1973 and had Michael two years later.

As we prepared for marriage, we had to deal with the difficult issue of intermarriage. Rabbis in the Orthodox and Conservative branches of Judaism refuse to perform a marriage ceremony between a Jew and a non-Jew. Today, nearly half of the two thousand Reform rabbis will officiate, provided the couple agrees to raise Jewish children.

When the Reform rabbi in Columbia wouldn't marry us, he referred us to Rabbi Norman Goldberg of Augusta, Georgia. Rabbi Goldberg learned ecumenism while growing up in Quincy, Illinois. Not having a synagogue nearby, his father took him to visit Catholic and Protestant churches. The friendly atmosphere between the various denominations and racial groups paved the way for his liberal mindset later in life. In 1969, Rabbi Goldberg wrote *The Rabbi and Mr. McGillicutty*, an informal guide for ministers and rabbis. Patrick J. McGillicutty, the imaginary secretary, dictated the book.

Steve and I met Rabbi Goldberg at the Wade Hampton Hotel, a Columbia landmark later razed to make room for the AT&T building. We walked through the art deco lobby to a restaurant called Maxim's and recognized him immediately because he wore his yarmulke, or Jewish skullcap. With slightly receding hair and horn-rimmed glasses, the rabbi had a pleasant, professorial look. His first words were, "Which one of you is the Jew and which one of you is the Greek?" We had a hearty laugh because to him Steve looked more Jewish than I did.

Smiling, I said, "To tell you the truth, when Steve first saw me, he thought I was an Arab. I belonged to the International Society and had lots of Mid-Eastern friends."

The rabbi said, "Well, we're all from the same neck of the woods when you really get down to it. Let me just start by saying that I'm truly honored that you chose me to officiate at your wedding. I've done many of these, and I'd like to share a bit of my philosophy if I could.

"Because it's a big, diverse world, Jews and non-Jews will inevitably fall in love. Interfaith couples come in all shapes and sizes. I'm always encouraged that marriages like yours increase cultural and religious understanding. Steve, from what I understand, you and Gail have agreed to raise your children Jewish?"

Nodding, Steve said, "Yes."

"Well, that's half the battle, so you're ahead of the game. Let's talk a minute about what unites and divides you—values aside from religion such as political, cultural, or regional differences."

Steve said, "It's interesting that you brought that up. I recently referred to us as a 'mixed couple' because I'm from the North and Gail's from the South. My family couldn't even believe there were Jews down here."

The rabbi said, "You might find it interesting that the liberal conservative divide within the same religion is actually more difficult to overcome than crossing the divide between totally different religions. Enough of that. Steve, tell me more about your family."

Steve said, "Well, both of my grandparents came over from small villages in Greece and Turkey. They were first generation and stressed the importance of education and achievement. Dad graduated from MIT and served in the Navy. I went to Greek Sunday School, but I never heard them say they wanted me to marry a Greek girl. I presume they believed in God, but I never asked them. Their divorce, when I was a freshman in college, caused a lot of turmoil."

The rabbi asked, "Tell me, Steve, did you ever think about converting?"

"No, not seriously. I'd have to learn more about my own religion first," he said.

Looking at me, the rabbi asked, "Gail, does it bother you? Would you prefer it if Steve converted?"

"No. I guess if I were more religious, I would have pushed for it."

The rabbi said, "Your differences remind me of the Hanukkah story when the Maccabees fought the Greeks around 165 BC. Just think about it—two rich cultures offering so much to the world.

"I'd like to give you some insight about the two mindsets. Jews don't need to prove God. They know by faith that he exists. Greeks, on the other hand, need to prove everything. If they can't prove something, it doesn't exist. It may not apply to you now, but you never know. If somewhere down the line one of you becomes religious, it could explain the differences."

When the conversation ended, we said goodbye with the understanding that if we had further questions, we could call and ask for another meeting.

On August 3, 1973, Steve and I, along with Janna, Laurie, Mom, Dad, and both my grandmothers, drove to Augusta, where Rabbi Goldberg's married us in a Jewish ceremony. I wore a long, pink chiffon dress with free-flowing sleeves. Steve's sister, Susan, who lived in London, sent yellow roses. Their parents remained in separate locations in Europe.

Mom and Dad initially wanted me to marry someone Jewish, but when they got to know Steve they expressed elation over my choice. Over the years, they said, "Steve is the son we never had." They admired the way he moved confidently within the Jewish and larger legal communities. For years, Dad relied on Steve's lawyerly expertise in real estate. Steve owes his adaptability to his remarkable parents, Steve and Lela, both of whom grew up in New Haven, Connecticut, among an eclectic mix of ethnic friends.

Despite wanting to raise my children Jewish, I never envisioned living in an insular world, Jewish or Christian. In cosmopolitan DC, intermarried couples moved in a variety of social circles. In Columbia, however, Jews and Christians didn't mix. As one of only a few intermarried couples, I felt isolated. Though discouraging intermarriage reflects the Jewish instinctive desire for self-preservation, it often has the effect of reverse snobbery. Ultimately, feeling more comfortable with my Jewish friends, we joined Tree of Life Congregation, a Reform synagogue, where Michael later had his bar mitzvah.

Coming home gave me a chance to build strong relationships with Janna and Laurie. Because we recognized the drawbacks of Mom's Pollyanna atmosphere, the three of us cultivated an unstudied chumminess marked by honesty, humor, and even a healthy dose of sarcasm. Our camaraderie comes from having picked one another up many times after falling. Together, we've confronted divorce, the death of a loved one, and concerns over children, husbands, and in-laws. Today, with any sign of a problem, we visit or pray over the phone. Though staying close requires keeping a watchful eye for unresolved issues, I trust them with my life and find it well worth the effort.

CHAPTER 8

Motherhood

Family stories grow to be bigger than the experiences themselves.
They become home to us, tell us who we are and who we want to
be. Over the years, they take on more and more embellishment
and adornments until they eclipse the actual memories. They become our past—just as a snapshot will, at first, enhance a memory,
then replace it.

—Judy Goldman, *Losing My Sister*[1]

AFTER MICHAEL WAS BORN, I developed a new level of empathy. I realized
that behind every odious or pitiful individual stood a mother more or less
like me, agonizing and worrying. Identifying with the larger world in this
way led to a dramatic shift in my personality. I realized that the line separating any of us amounts to a thin veil of luck.

Looking through an old scrapbook, I found a picture of Michael in
preschool. Donning his new Superman T-shirt, he looked to have taken on
the Man of Steel's persona—laser-like invincible eyes and matchless confidence. I'm taken back to the day I took it.

While I waited for him to arrive from school, I walked into the backyard to replenish the bird feeders. When the doorbell rang, I ran to greet
him and asked, "How was your day, honey? Did they like your new T-shirt?"

"Yes," he said.

"What do you want for lunch?" I asked.

"Maybe just half of a peanut butter and jelly sandwich. Someone
brought in birthday cake so I'm not very hungry."

The two of us moved into the den where we sat on a blue-plaid sofa
with a clear view to the backyard. Seeing that the squirrels were tearing

---

1. Goldman, *Losing My Sister*, 1593.

into the bird food, I said, "Michael, at this rate, the birds won't have anything to eat."

He said, "We need to trick the squirrels, Mama. Let's grease the pole so they can't get to the seeds."

"Michael, that's a great idea." I got a can of Crisco, placed a stool under the feeder, and let him effect the ruse.

Watching the squirrels try to conquer that slippery pole made for great sport. After a few minutes of laughter, Michael said, "Mom, let's take of picture of the squirrels falling. Quick! Get Dad's camera."

We didn't catch any squirrels in freefall that day, but I got an especially good shot of Michael, one that serves as a reminder of better times. For years, I prayed over it, asking God to restore the ebullient, self-satisfied expression on his face.

Another fond memory centers on the hours Michael and I spent reading his picture dictionary after lunch. I can still visualize his beautifully formed hands and inquisitive brown eyes as he peppered me with a thousand questions. What I remember most was his innocent expectation that I had at my fingertips every piece of knowledge regarding his burgeoning universe.

Every night before bedtime, Michael picked a TV show suitable for the three of us to watch together. One evening, as we watched a *Batman* sequence, Michael, began screaming. "Help," he said, "I can't see the TV." Steve and I, glaring at each other, assumed he was joking.

Seeing his tears and elevating panic, I asked, "Michael, what is it, honey? Rub your eyes. You must have gotten something in them."

We watched as he stood and groped his way to the bathroom. To our horror, he bumped into the den wall and fell hard to the floor. We heard a loud thump when his head took the brunt of the impact.

Grabbing his forehead, he shrieked, "Someone please help me. How in the world am I supposed to get around? Get me to a hospital right away. I need to see a doctor!"

Scared out of our wits, Steve and I ran in several directions looking for the keys. After helping Michael up, we guided him to the car.

After Steve started the car, I said, "Wait! We can't go yet. I have to call his pediatrician. He can meet us at the hospital and save time."

Michael said, "No, don't do that. We need to go now!"

As the car moved out of the driveway, we heard a boisterous squeal of delight. In between breathless peals of laughter, Michael said, "I just can't believe y'all. I got you good this time."

With great skill, he had faked the entire episode. I bopped him all over in sheer frustration and relief, realizing that he deserved an Academy Award. He came by it naturally—a chip off the old block of his great-grandfather, Gus.

Another practical joke involved Mom. Due in part to her generosity, Jewish Family Services had begun to resettle Russian Jewish immigrants in our community. Employing his great skill at mimicry, Michael called Mom on the phone and took on the persona of a Jewish Russian immigrant. He almost had her convinced that she wasn't giving her fair share when he made the mistake of telling her that her Russian ancestors would be ashamed. At this point, realizing the ruse, the two of them bellowed in amusement.

I had always assumed the best when I envisioned my future rolling out. Mom's fanciful vision had its drawbacks when taken to extremes, but at least it left the impression of a tidy, ordered universe with a degree of rough-hewn justice. When our difficulties began, this expectation and everything associated with it shattered into a million disjointed shards.

The first sign of trouble was Michael's obstinate refusal to cooperate. His pattern of compulsive overeating disturbed every sense of order and routine. He gained a great deal of weight, something Steve and I micromanaged inappropriately.

When Michael's antics disrupted the Hebrew class, his teacher called to say, "Michael's behavior prevents me from teaching the essentials of Jewish values." She couldn't have leveled any worse criticism.

Coming from an ultra-polite, respectable family six feet above reproach, I knew precious little about boys misbehaving and even less about malicious tongues wagging behind my back. I grieved for our dear boy, knowing that depression stood as the root cause of his acting out. I was jealous of those with perfect families who knew nothing about the vagaries of fate and how depression can strike anyone at any time.

Meanwhile, an impossible secret, like a rogue piece of the puzzle, hung in the air like a pernicious ghost. Our family wouldn't know the root cause of our hapless lot for over two decades.

Michael's response:

It angers me that my reputation followed me to Heathwood. That no doubt had an effect on how I was treated and in turn behaved. I never felt like I was treated fairly there. I never felt like my teachers liked me. If you expect a kid to be a problem, you're going to treat him differently. I'm sure I picked up on some of that unfairness and acted out.

In grammar school, Michael never expressed in so many words that he felt depressed. Sadly, his state of mind felt so ordinary that he had nothing to compare it with. One morning, unable to get ready for school, he said, "I just feel sick, Mom."

Though he didn't have a fever, it was pointless to force his hand.

When the phone rang, I answered it in my bedroom. A voice said, "Gail, this is Moira. Can you meet me at the Waffle House? I need to talk to you about something important." Moira was a friend and not one of my favorites, but I thought it would do me good to get out. At this point, I hadn't shared with her anything about Michael's depression.

Looking in on Michael, I hugged him goodbye, and instructed Ana, our housekeeper, to keep an eye on him.

Moira had already ordered when I sat down. I ordered a large vegetable omelet and got right to the point. I asked, "What's wrong, Moira? You sounded like it was urgent."

She said, "Jake has just been accepted to three Ivy League colleges. They're competing for him, and he's feeling a lot of pressure about the decision."

I said, "Well, that's a nice problem to have, isn't it? How long does he have before deciding?"

"A month," she said. "He woke up crying this morning. I haven't seen him like this in years. Don't they say, 'You're only as happy as your unhappiest child?'"

When her cell phone rang, I heard her say, "Jake, don't worry. I'll be there in five minutes." Without explaining, she grabbed her purse and left without paying her portion of the bill.

Eating alone, I could hardly contain my red-hot anger. Moira had no right to her breast-beating. My pain was significantly worse. Suddenly, I hated the expression, "You're only as happy as your unhappiest child." Let her live out the notion. For me, continuing to do so would mean my downfall. Was mother love inherently co-dependent and without boundaries?

I had visions of staving off the instinct and cauterizing forever. The mere suggestion of this, like a python, wrapped itself around my mind, spelling poisonous doom.

I returned home, trying not to over-identify with Michael's mood. I hugged him, saying, "Michael, I love you so much. Do you want to talk to me about anything?"

He said, "Nothing's wrong. I love you, too, Mama. Will you please read *The Fire Cat*?"

Both of us had practically memorized it.

Pickles the cat had too much time on his hands and no occupation. He lived in a barrel. Because he had nothing to do, he started bullying the other cats. Mrs. Goodkind, recognizing his isolation, turned his life around.

She arranged to have him adopted by the Hook and Ladder Company, where he became a full-fledged member of the fire department. He learned how to slide down the pole, sit on the fire truck, rush to fires, and show kindness to the other cats. The story ends with Pickles climbing up a tree to save a cat that he once bullied.

Michael wanted me to read his favorite part again: "Pickles, you are not a bad cat. You are not a good cat. You are good and bad, and bad and good. You are a mixed-up cat. What you need is a good home. Then you will be good."[2]

As I closed the book, a familiar sadness descended. Mystified about Michael's attachment to Pickles' story of redemption, I feared he needed a Mrs. Goodkind and not me.

2. Averill, *Fire Cat*, 8.

CHAPTER 9

Jewish Life

HAVING A DIRE NEED for diversion, in 1982, I agreed to serve on the board of Hadassah with Mom. My involvement in Jewish life increased my awareness of the communal bond known as Jewish geography. I felt six degrees of separation every time I met someone who knew about my parents' early years.

I know of two families in which the fathers attended college together, appeared as groomsmen in each other's weddings, and remained close throughout the years of raising their children. Though the paternal grandfathers never met, they felt a common bond through association. One grandfather survived Ebensee, the concentration camp in Austria, the other liberated the very same camp. The survivor discovered this only when reading the fine print of the liberator's obituary. He had tried unsuccessfully to locate this very man over most of his life, never knowing of their son's friendship.

A friend of mine overheard a poignant conversation between two elderly Jewish men visiting their grandchildren in Columbia. Making small talk, they soon realized that, remarkably, they were from the same *shtetl*, or village, in Russia. Overjoyed by the coincidence, they exchanged bountiful hugs. Then, one turned to the other and said, "Can you actually believe we lived to see the day when the czars aren't in control?"

Growing up, Mom appeared to align herself with any judgment and opinion Columbia's Jewish community held. Her many offhand comments about how this or that favored friend thought so much of me left the impression that, above all things, she valued the opinion of others. I witnessed a different side of Mom's personality when we attended our first Hadassah board meeting.

The gathering assembled at the home of Mom's good friend Marlene. An architectural knockout, the house stood between a lake and a large woodland tract. Once inside, I could see the full panoply of fall colors reflected in crystal-clear waters. I recognized the chic transitional style of Pulliam Morris, the finest design firm in Columbia.

As we made our way into the kitchen for coffee, my eyes lit on an exquisite, burnished gold menorah on the étagère. Thinking it was a family heirloom, I said, "Marlene, tell me the story behind this gorgeous piece."

She said, "Oh, it's from the Tiffany collection. If you want one, I can give your mom the catalog." Then she whispered, "Better yet, I'll give the catalogue to you. Maybe you girls can buy her one as a Hanukkah present this year."

I said, "That's a great idea."

We socialized for a few more minutes before moving into the living room. The meeting occurred soon after the Sabra and Shatila massacre in Lebanon. Barbara, the president, called the meeting to order, saying, "In light of the current situation in Israel, I'd like to dispense with normal business. As many of you may know, a scathing op-ed piece appeared in the *New York Times* yesterday attacking Israel."

The September 16, 1982 *Times* article stated that the Israeli military allowed a right-wing Lebanese militia to enter two Palestinian refugee camps in Beirut. In the ensuing three-day rampage, the militia, linked to the Maronite Christian Phalange Party, raped, killed, and dismembered at least eight hundred civilians while Israeli flares illuminated the camps' narrow and darkened alleyways. Nearly all the dead were women, children, and elderly men.[1]

Barbara said, "We need to present a united front in countering the liberal press. The *Times* article indicated that Sharon misled American officials who voiced concern about the safety of civilians in the camps."

"Wait a minute," Mom interjected. "There's mounting uproar even in Israel. If they can criticize Sharon, why can't we?"

Julia, the secretary, said, "Let's face it, Pat. Anti-Semitism motivates most public opinion here. If we agree with them, we'll play into their hands."

Mom countered by saying, "I think you're wrong. The Israeli Lobby has already caused a backlash. The Senate was once the greatest debating body in the world. Now, people don't speak their mind for fear of being called anti-Semitic. I can criticize Israel the way I criticize my child, because I love her so. If we support Israel blindly, the Jewish community will lose all

---

1. Friedman and *Times*, "Beirut Massacre."

credibility. In the long run, it will bring about more misunderstanding and even greater anti-Semitism."

A palling silence saturated the air. Mina, the treasurer, said, "Pat, I have to say, I'm disappointed that you feel the way you do."

Quickly, Barbara interjected, saying, "Pat, I know of your strong love for Israel. We just have a difference of opinion here. If you don't mind, I'd like to remind you that it's a very old issue. Sometimes domestic debate gives enemies of Israel fuel for their own views."

Mom said, "Thanks, Barbara. At least you validate my commitment. I understand your point of view, but I wholeheartedly disagree with it. We need healthy debate, both here and in Israel."

We had to leave early, but Marlene told us the discussion continued for another hour. Though I didn't express my opinion at the meeting, I agreed with Mom.

Because of the dissension her views caused, Mom decided not to chair the fundraising drive that year. Despite their differing opinions, Mom and her Hadassah cohorts remained devoted until the time of her death.

In 1995, I gave Mom a poem I wrote on the occasion of Prime Minister Rabin's assassination. It had the inscription, "I love and respect the way you love Israel." She framed it and placed it in her vanity.

Jerusalem

As the noonday brightness fades, a soft glow follows evening shade.

City of light on a distant hill, your transparent gold flickering still,

Jerusalem, when shall I return?

A nation's love born in eternity of ancient memory and soulful quest,

only now being shamed by a blood-stained breast.

Your peaceful refrain no more, Jerusalem, I thought I knew you.

Whether a place of national appeal or, beyond time, a mystic ideal

Your light, however dim, still steadies the course, ably reflecting

our common source

Jerusalem, when shall I return?

CHAPTER 10

Reckoning and Restoration

MOM AND I HAD each benefitted from individual therapy and knew full well the importance of letting down barriers and defense mechanisms. We could admit to our failings and even laugh about our rage-filled years. Discussing our defining pattern of enmeshment and resistance, we concluded that my rebellion served a healthy purpose.

I assumed we had no more issues to resolve, but flashbacks, like the miasma of unpleasant memory, began to surface. Though bringing up unfinished business would pose a risk, I knew I had to discuss a certain family dynamic that had caused me considerable pain.

I arrived at their house, one morning, to find Dad at work and Mom resting in bed. I rarely saw the bedroom in the light of early morning. Open French doors let in a chorus of birdsong—high-pitched flute calls, silver bells, and harp peals. Miniature roses on the chintz drapery took on dawn's opalescent glow.

When I gave Mom a bear hug, I caught a whiff of her lavender-and-almond hand cream. She wore her favorite nightgown, a long aqua silk with blue appliquéd flowers down the front. Remembering the robins nesting on her porch, she suddenly rose to check on their progress. For weeks, we had witnessed the unfolding natural drama of a mother robin laying and hatching three eggs. Afterward, both parents engaged in a fast and furious feeding program.

I heard her exclaim from the porch, "Help, Gail. There're only two birds in the nest. One of them must have fallen." Spotting it on the floor, she said, "Oh my God, I could have stepped on it."

Gingerly, she picked up the fledgling bird and cupped it in her hands. Devastated at having to return it to its nest, her expression showed a mixture of motherly affection and pitiable pain.

44

I sensed in the porch scenario a microcosm of the many years Mom spent overseeing her own brood of three. Seeing the male robin play such an active role in parenting hit a raw nerve. At least in the animal kingdom, the female didn't have to invite the male to get involved.

With the fledgling back in its nest and Mom dressed for the day, we decided to make tea. Setting everything aside for this favored ritual made our conversations seem more intentional. I took out the cinnamon spice as Mom sliced the lemons.

At the table, Mom commented on the beautiful view from her window. We had both endured the stultifying heat and humidity of summer and welcomed fall. She said, "I just love the long shadows. It feels like something in the air has changed, even though the temperature is the same."

She picked up a pair of binoculars and began spotting and naming birds.

When she saw a cardinal, Mudge's favorite, she said, "Oh, Gail, I almost forgot." She brought in a framed poem that Mudge wrote years ago. After showing where she wanted to hang it, she read it aloud:

> Little red bird as you fly past my window swiftly by
>
> Your plumage and emblazonry of life's ardent fervency
>
> You never stop, you never pause. Is it little bird, because
>
> You know too as well as I your semblance is a fallacy
>
> That all one's life can never be one glad pursuit of ecstasy.

I asked, "Mom, do you ever wonder what secrets Mudge took with her? I've always gotten the impression that she didn't tell us all."

"I wonder about that myself," she said.

A prism attached to the windowsill cast a rainbow on the adjacent wall. Of its own accord, it began swinging from side to side. As we stared at it, mesmerized at this breaking in of new energy, I seized the moment.

I said, "Mom, I need to bring up something personal. Do you mind? It's about Dad."

"Well, sure, honey, fire away," she said.

"You've always been there for me, but I needed both of you to parent me. I know Dad is naturally reserved, but sometimes he seems uncomfortable showing his affection for me."

"Why would you think that, honey?"

I paused, wondering if I should continue. "The truth is, Mom, maybe he senses you are possessive. I don't understand it, because the two of you have always been so close. I hope you don't get upset with me." I paused, afraid to continue.

"Go ahead, honey. You need to talk."

"Well, I hope you don't mind if I ask, is there a part of you that wants to keep Dad all to yourself?" I recall a gentle smile of recognition. Concentrating on the fact that I had finally spoken scary words, nothing else she may have said registered.

I grabbed her hands in mine, saying, "Mom, I think we've come full circle. We're almost like sisters now, instead of mother and daughter." Her touch on my shoulder left an impression of such exquisite pleasure that I hoped to retain its imprint.

For more than forty years, we spent long afternoons together, listening to music and whispering visions never to be untold or unseen. Our intimacy opened her up in such a way that I no longer had to interpret or second-guess her feelings. She shared one enlightening insight after another. Once, she said, "Even in healthy, enduring relationships, jealousy can rear its ugly head. It's completely normal and compatible with love. It only creates havoc when it's not expressed. Feelings shouldn't be judged. They're always legitimate."

This awareness had a positive impact on my spiritual life. It told me that I could take every sentiment, good or bad, to a God who wouldn't judge me.

Later in life, I asked her how she managed to give each of her many friends the same caliber of love and affection.

She responded, "Honey, love is a wellspring. The more you give, the more you have to give."

Once, when Steve and I drove to her house, he delighted in a curious phenomenon. He said, "You seem to have a special antenna for your Mom. Even a mile away, you start acting like her."

My renewed relationship with Mom served as a counterpoint to my other worries. I wondered whether my life, one fraught with peril and anxiety, could also contain possibility. I considered that the universe might have other riches in store for me.

CHAPTER 11

Spirituality in Judaism

MICHAEL'S PROBLEMS PERSISTED THROUGHOUT grammar school, causing me to dread teacher conferences and wince every time a classmate's mother called. Perhaps unaware of what was working on me, I made a decision that some may have considered counterintuitive—that of taking part in a community-wide Holocaust study. Though my path was circuitous, I was searching for spiritual answers. The course consisted of group discussion and lecture material. I joined in as we analyzed films, historical commentaries, novels, and personal accounts. When watching the documentary *Shoah*, an all-consuming fear overcame me at the idea of living alone in an absurd and meaningless universe.

Because of college reading that deconstructed and debunked religion, I had little confidence in rational thought as a means to reach God. Freud explained belief by citing unmet father needs or wish fulfillment.[1] Albert Camus wrote of the devastating consequences of life without God, often with greater insight than any theologian could. In *The Myth of Sisyphus*, he stated that there was only one serious philosophical issue: not whether to commit suicide but when.[2]

After the study, I found myself peddling aimlessly in place with no purpose. Having increased sensitivity to suffering in general, I found it difficult to watch the news or read the newspaper. Instances of injustice previously brushed aside in my mind became a point of focus. I wondered where people found the strength of character to overcome dire circumstances. In truth, I didn't know where I would find the strength to overcome mine.

My preoccupation with hard issues proved to be a necessary phase in a healthy spiritual process. During this time, I happened to read a quote from

1. Freud and Gay, *Future of Illusion*.
2. Camus, *Modern Classics*, 51.

47

C. S. Lewis's *Mere Christianity* in which he explained how he resolved his main objection to faith: the cruelty in the universe.

> Thus in the very act of trying to prove that God did not exist—in other words, that the whole of reality was senseless—I was forced to assume that one part of reality—namely my sense of justice—was full of sense. If the whole universe has no meaning, I should never have found out . . . just as if there was no light in the universe and therefore no creatures with eyes, I should not have known it was dark. Dark would be without meaning.[3]

As I absorbed Lewis's logic, my heart began to loosen and give way to a profound yearning for God. Admitting that the material world alone could not sustain me, I began an extensive course of reading. I soon learned that man has a spiritual alternative completely alien to the mindset of postmodern philosophy.

Remembering Rabbi Goldberg's insight, I could see a difference between two worldviews. The Hebrew mindset assumes God's existence from the existential fact of being in relationship with him. Greek thought, which is the foundation of Western philosophy, seeks to prove God through logic and reasoned analysis.

Though Rabbi Abraham Joshua Heschel, Martin Buber, and Franz Rosenzweig had advanced degrees in philosophy, their ideas appeared to take God's existence for granted. My skepticism at the time required the logical approach of the Greeks.

I read in the field of natural theology, a branch of philosophy examining the world for empirical evidence of God. I focused on the cosmological origins of the universe, moral law, the philosophy behind miracles, and the argument from desire.

Mine was the slow prodding search of a skeptic. I learned that atheism left too many unanswered questions. Approximately a year into my study, I found my mind in a radically different place. I began to doubt my very doubts and became less resistant to a supernatural reality. Though far from understanding how God's love mysteriously enables hope, I reasoned that my intense longing for him signaled the best evidence for his existence.

When I began accessing intuitive truths alongside the provable scientific ones, my personality shifted to a new center. My heart, mind, and soul coalesced, and I began praying to the personal God of the Bible. I saw the

---

3. Lewis, *Mere Christianity*, 38.

difference between a theory about God and a personal relationship with him. I had come full circle.

Rabbi Heschel's notion of "divine pathos," God's emotional involvement in the life of his people, became critical to my understanding of the Hebrew Scriptures. Heschel emphasized the importance of living in awe, a state of radical amazement in which we take nothing for granted.[4]

Buber wrote of the difference between knowing about God and knowing him directly. Buber explored communication by defining two fundamental relationships: I-It and I-Thou. In the latter, one fully engages with the other in authentic dialogue. Buber experienced the profundity of this in his encounter with God and his fellow man.[5]

Rosenzweig wrote that Judaism consists of a personal existential decision in which a Jew connects not only to God but also to the entire covenantal group of Israel. Through observance, a Jew participates in the great dance of survival, evoking the mystery of Israel's election.[6] Despite my knowledge that observance entails more than dry legalism, I had little desire to immerse myself on this level. Here, I could identify with Buber's non-observant path. Buber contended that the soul of Judaism rests in the righteous faith of the patriarchs long before the law was given.[7]

I soon developed a close friendship with David Miller, a Holocaust survivor living in Columbia. Over the years, I saw how his substantive faith enabled him cope with his past.

Mr. Miller, along with five thousand resistance fighters, participated in the Warsaw Ghetto uprising that began on April 19, 1943. He was captured and sent to Auschwitz. In April 1945, he escaped by pushing aside a guard and fleeing into the woods. He eventually made his way to the American Liberation soldiers. After the war, he went to Landsburg, a displaced persons' camp, in Germany.

Once he regained his strength, he learned of the death of his mother, father, and three sisters. He also met another survivor, his future wife, Cela. In 1949, a few months after their wedding, they received notice that Beth Shalom Synagogue in Columbia would sponsor them.

---

4. Kimelman, "Theology of Abraham."
5. Moberly, "Knowing God."
6. Herberg, "Rosenzweig's 'Judaism.'"
7. Buber, *Two Types.*

Once, sitting next to Mr. Miller in synagogue, I was transported by his simple piety and spirituality. His presence imparted divine calm and deep surrender, enabling me to override my tenuous Hebrew.

In my frequent visits to Mr. Miller's house, I sought solace from him. Because psychological testing put Michael in the gifted category, his poor performance baffled both his teachers and us. Without the resources for detention, the school had no means of making him accountable. Unfortunately, the onus fell on Steve and me, something that caused frequent battles.

CHAPTER 12

Growing Dissatisfaction

SPIRITUAL JUDAISM ELEVATED ME far above the secularism I had grown up with. It expanded the boundaries of my heart and opened me to an unseen reality. When I found the synagogue experience disappointing, I took refuge in prayer and reading the Tanakh. Rather than encountering legalism, I uncovered kernels of grace that would soon come into fruition.

Meanwhile, I watched as despondency enveloped Michael, settling into his mind and sucking the lifeblood out of his personality. His eyes betrayed what he couldn't or wouldn't express. I feared that he might prefer death than to wake up another day.

Because Judaism had never answered my questions about life's injustice, I reached a plateau in which it could no longer satisfy me. When an impenetrable fog began separating me from God, my prayer life turned dry and shallow. I wondered whether God was simply absent or just hidden. Assuming that I'd missed a critical piece of the Jewish spiritual puzzle, I delved deeper. I read Eli Wiesel's book *Night*. Several friends in my Holocaust study had spoken of its power, but I had neglected reading it.

In a gripping section, Wiesel described how the Nazis hung two men and a boy on a gallows for stealing a cache of guns. They forced thousands to witness as the men died and the boy lingered in torturous agony for more than a half hour. Wiesel wrote that the boy had the sad face of a little angel. When someone rhetorically asked, "Where is God?," Wiesel responded, "Where is he? He is hanging here on the gallows." God, for Wiesel, was dead.[1]

Instead of providing the enlightenment I'd hoped for, Wiesel's chronicle added fuel to my fiery angst. Knowing that the prophets had struggled with God, I focused on a passage in Isaiah (63:9):

1. Wiesel and Wiesel, *Night*, 158.

In all their affliction he was afflicted,

and the angel of his presence saved them;

in his love and in his pity he redeemed them;

he lifted them up and carried them all the days of old.

Simone Weil, a philosopher who was born into a secular Jewish family and later found herself drawn to Christianity, wrote about the category of affliction in which we wait for God and get no response. In *Waiting for God,* she described this pain as private and isolating, biting the substance of a soul more than mere physical suffering. Despite God's infinitude, I reasoned that God could not contain, encompass, or override my particular condition.[2]

I understood the Jewish concept of divine pathos as the one harmonic chord representing God's suffering love. Yet a festering anxiety plagued me. How could God possibly fathom the depth of my angst? Terence E. Fretheim in *The Suffering of God* wrote that because we are made in God's image we have permission to reverse the process and know God's nature. God cannot know human attributes such as sexuality, sin, and guilt.[3]

With great vexation of soul, I realized that spiritual despair fit this very category. Despite God's infinitude, I reasoned that God could not contain, encompass, or override my particular angst. I reached a divide that caused my entire framework to crumble. My relationship with God came to a standstill. I would have preferred torture to the cold, vaulted emptiness that lay waste to my interior. As part of some otherworldly conundrum, I longed for the Almighty to experience the ultimate psychic insult of separation from God. Nothing else would satisfy.

During this time, I remained close to Glen and Linda Welsford, my evangelical friends. They knew of my love for Judaism but not of my growing dissatisfaction. Once, I made a curious request of Glen. I said, "I know how much Jesus means to you, but I'd appreciate it if you and Linda wouldn't pray for me. It's a boundary issue and an invasion of my privacy."

He said, "Well, Gail, I didn't know you thought so highly of prayer."

Deflecting it with a glib remark, I left before extracting a promise.

I recalled the day I found Yancey's *Where is God When it Hurts?*, in which he recounted Wiesel's experience of watching the young boy die on the noose. Identifying with Wiesel's anger, Yancey went on to suggest that

2. Weil, *Awaiting God.*

3. Frethheim, *Suffering of God,* 11.

Jesus, in giving his life on Calvary, hung on the gallows alongside the young boy.[4] While this provided food for thought, I let the idea languish. First, I wanted to explore two stumbling blocks—Christian anti-Semitism and the exclusivity of salvation espoused in Christianity.

A question our community rightly asks is, "If Christianity is true, why has it produced such bad fruit for the Jewish people?" The rationalization that anti-Semitic Christians couldn't have been authentic believers no longer worked for me. A cursory reading of church history revealed that many otherwise-devout church fathers spewed hatred toward the Jews. I also found it implausible to suggest that evil gets more publicity than good, that the quiet deeds and kindnesses performed by sincere Christians throughout the centuries somehow evened the score.

I wanted a degree of clarity as to how something so pure in origin could have been perverted in such a diabolical way. The only conclusion that provided some satisfaction came from Karl Stern's understanding of the dialectical relationship between good and evil. Stern, in *The Pillar of Fire,* noted their symbiotic pairing in revelation history, with evil feeding off the good. When God revealed himself at Sinai, the Israelites below engaged in the evil of idol worship below.[5]

Even while Jesus walked the earth, the forces of evil worked to obscure his message. Ultimately, the battle between good and evil plays out within each human heart. A great man or movement can succumb to a fatal flaw— be it anti-Semitism or some other heinous quirk.

I struggled to reconcile the narrowness of salvation found in Christianity with the wideness of God's mercy at its core. Though this exclusivity affects others apart from the Jews, my problem centered on a singular comparison: According to Christianity's concept of grace, Hitler, in a last- minute formulation, could gain entrance into heaven while the Jewish children he victimized would be in hell. I considered that Orthodox Jews, waiting for the Messiah as they understood him, could show more faith than nominal Christians sitting in the pews every Sunday.

Respected Christian theologians such as C. S. Lewis, John Stott, N. T. Wright, Dallas Willard, and Billy Graham helped me to see a way forward. My interest in the fate of the sincere nonbeliever motivated me to read Lewis in the first place. God used my particular interest to love, mold, and sculpt me into belief, with little change in my liberal sensibility.

4. Yancey, *Where Is God?*
5. Stern, *Pillar of Fire,* 242.

As my struggle played out, I shared more with the Welsfords—even, in a reversal, asking for prayer. They had an unreserved love for the Jewish people and disdained any form of religious bigotry. Glen regularly attended the Saturday morning service at Beth Shalom Synagogue. On a trip to Jerusalem, he donned Michael's prayer shawl at the Western Wailing Wall as a token of our mutual affection.

As we discussed my stumbling blocks, I could see that Linda and Glen held to the conservative view regarding salvation. In lively, provocative exchanges, they explained how their belief had an impact on their social and political views. Though the shape of our faith would come to differ, their relationship with Jesus piqued my imagination. In the solemn interstice of doubt, I gleaned that Jesus was more than an abstraction, but one connected to personhood and hope.

Glen suggested that I read Mortimer Adler's *Truth in Religion*. Basing his view on the Greek logic of non-contradiction, Adler stated that two opposing views could not both contain equal truth. Though he affirmed his faith in tolerance and plurality, he contended that of the three Western religions claiming revelatory truth only one could be entirely true. The others only approximated it and contained mistakes or falsehoods.[6]

I juxtaposed Adler's understanding with Heschel's view of polarity and paradox. Heschel stated that the point is not either-or but both-and. For example, the dichotomy between transcendence and immanence is an oversimplification: God remains transcendent in his immanence and immanent in his transcendence. Because such paradoxical words cut both ways, he called them "scissors words."[7] Though paradox had benefitted much of my emotional thinking up to this point, I questioned whether two contradictory ideas could contain equal truth.

Rosensweig, who conceded the truthfulness of Christianity, decided against conversion. Believing that Judaism and Christianity were two perspectives of one reality, he wrote, "God's truth is one but for man, it is irreducibly split since the truth as men see it is conditioned by one's community of faith."[8] Because I held to Adler's view of non-contradiction, I could not accept Rosensweig's statement.

Rabbi Irving Greenberg stated that because the truth of Jesus' messiahship will be known at the end of days, the dispute should be tabled.

6. Adler, *Truth in Religion*, 36.
7. Kimelman, "Theology of Abraham."
8. Frunză, "Aspects of Connection."

When the day arrives, Jews and Christians can ask Jesus whether this is his first coming or his second. Greenberg never suggested that both positions could be true.[9]

Jacob Neusner, in *A Rabbi Talks with Jesus,* brought the issue home to me. He conceded that Jesus claimed that he was the dwelling place of the divine.[10] Neusner subsequently corresponded with Pope Benedict on this point and, despite differences, they became friends. The Pope appreciated that Neusner was the first Jewish theologian to expose the issue at the heart of the debate—that Jesus understood himself as the Torah, the word of God in person.[11]

During this interval, Michael, seeing my books lying around, asked, "Mom, why are you reading all this? Are you confused or something?"

I said, "I know you've been unhappy for a long time. I'm reading books that show me how God suffers alongside us." Because he was nearing his bar mitzvah, I didn't offer details. I wouldn't reveal my faith to him until he reached high school.

One night, in a hurry to get to a PTA meeting at Michael's school, I decided to wash my hair in the bathroom sink. I gathered the essentials and filled the basin. Lowering my head into the lukewarm water felt like submerging myself in a freshwater pond. When I looked up at broken tiles and faded green wallpaper, a lightness of spirit entered me. I prayed, "Jesus, if you're there, show me what you want me to see."

Over the next several years, I studied Jewish views related to the character of God, suffering, and evil. After comparing Jewish and Christian concepts on grace and atonement, I studied the evidence for the resurrection and ideas related to biblical interpretation.

My epiphany merged both logic and feeling. I worked through my reservations by praying, reflecting, and assimilating faith in small increments. A too-sudden conversion would have assaulted my psyche like a wrecking ball. Though the insights came gradually, some scarcely apprehended and others denied, they ultimately conquered my being: I experienced a complete transformation and reorientation of my soul.

9. Greenberg, "Jews Affirmed."

10. Neusner, *Rabbi Talks,* 30.

11. Neusner, "My Argument."

CHAPTER 13

Jewish Concepts Foreshadowing Christianity

MANY OF THE IDEAS I found in my studies pointed me in the direction of Christianity. It is common, if not typical, for Jewish scholars to lay heavy weight on the differences between Judaism and Christianity. Assuming the creed-deed paradigm, they emphasize Christianity's focus on faith and Judaism's focus on action. Yet both religions stress social action and ethical behavior. In fact, during the middle ages, Judaism held that salvation depended on one's acceptance of Maimonides' thirteen principles of faith.[1]

The Hebrew term for exile is *galut*. Though many Jewish prayers express a yearning for the return to the Jewish homeland, Arnold Eisen wrote that the concept of exile connotes more than physical displacement. Like original sin, it refers to an existential reality in which humans are alienated from innocence, from each other, and from God, himself. This exile affects the whole person and requires divine intercession for a change to occur.[2]

Despite their differences, the ultimate question for both Christians and Jews is, "How can a God who is both all-powerful and all-good allow evil to exist?" The conventional answer is that to destroy sin, God would need to limit our freedom. In such a world, we would resemble puppets, with God never knowing whether we freely gave our love for him.

Embedded in the biblical story is the hope that at the end of history, God will judge the wicked and reward the innocent who have suffered. Humans have an instinctive desire for all accounts to be settled—if not in this life, then certainly in the next. In *Rumor of Angels,* Peter Berger, a

---

1. Shapiro, "Maimonides' Thirteen Principles."
2. Kepnes, "'Turn Us to You.'"

sociologist of religion, wrote that some moral monstrosities not only cry out for justice but for damnation.[3]

Because evil's mystique often plays out on a grand cataclysmic scale, we find it unsettling to encounter it in our ordinary lives. In his poem "Herman Melville," W. H. Auden wrote, "Evil is unspectacular and always human, / And shares our bed and eats at our own table."[4]

I experienced this uncanny effect when touring Auschwitz with Steve. Thirty-five years old at the time, I had already begun my comparison study. I inhaled the frigid air and imagined the multitudes breathing in their last breath. Looking around me, I realized that the firmament had witnessed and partaken of monstrous evil.

As we readied to leave, the pilot went over instructions, Steve turned to me and asked, "Well, what did you think?" The only thing that came to my mind was, "It all seemed so ordinary."

The Jewish philosopher Philip Hallie, in his book *Lest Innocent Blood be Shed,* illustrated how goodness can overcome evil. After studying the institutional cruelty of the Holocaust, he fell into a deep depression. When he looked at the maiming of an innocent child with an indifferent eye, he began to think of himself as a monster.

On the verge of suicide, he found a chronicle about Huguenots in a German-occupied French village, Le Chambon Sur Lignon, who risked their lives to save more than five thousand Jewish children. As he read the account, he was overcome by tears, ones he later described as embodying moral praise and goodness in opposition to cruelty.[5]

The idea that we must ultimately acknowledge the mystery of suffering runs throughout Judaism and Christianity. God calls us to trust in his character, believe that his purposes, though mysterious, remain good. Some have suggested that our definition of good may differ from God's. Because we are limited in time, space, intelligence, and insight, we will never understand how God intends to redeem the world.

Much of Jewish thought relates to communal suffering, rather than individual suffering. The laments in Hebrew liturgy show the importance of contending with God as a nation. The book of Lamentations, read in emotional ceremonies, recites the horrors and atrocities during the long siege of Jerusalem and its aftermath.

3. Berger, *A Rumor.*
4. "Herman Melville."
5. Hallie, *Lest Innocent Blood.*

The most important insight I gained here, one key to my conversion, centered on the psychology of shared suffering. Psychologists note that shared pain focuses our egos and identities in significant ways.[6] In *Tragic Sense of Life*, Miguel de Unamuno referenced this when he noted that bodies are united in pleasure while souls are united in pain.[7]

I found a remarkable Jewish concept, dating from biblical times, affirming that the death of the righteous and innocent serves as an atonement for the sins of the nation and the world. The notion that God doesn't waste innocent suffering has helped the Jews to cope with their persecution over the centuries.[8] Though the rabbis who referenced this never had Jesus in mind, it illustrates the continuity between Jewish and Christian thought regarding the merits of shared or vicarious suffering.

Though the book of Job rejects the idea of suffering as punishment, Jewish literature records conflicting ideas. Maimonides, the twelfth century Jewish philosopher, stressing divine justice, believed that God always punishes sin.

It both frustrated and dismayed me that Judaism has such diametrically opposed views on the character of God. Rabbi Heschel believed that God suffers as much as we do, even more so because of his infinite consciousness.[9] His participating spirit elevates many amidst horrific circumstances. This divine-human partnership is woven into the thought of the prophets, the rabbis, and the mystical lore of kabbalah.

Maimonides, however, had a different view. Seeking to reconcile Judaism with Aristotelian philosophy, he contended that God has no emotion. Maimonides' Greek conception of God as the impassible, unmoved mover precluded my having a personal relationship with him.

The interplay between divine nearness and farness remains a constant theme in Jewish thought. In *Faith After the Holocaust*, Rabbi Eliezer Berkowits explores God's "hiddenness" as it appears in different contexts in the Hebrew Scriptures. He discusses the notion that God gave mankind over to their sin in the Holocaust.[10]

Heschel believed that God never hides, though we perceive that he does. Kabbalistic doctrine contends that God limited or contracted himself

6. Lomas, "Self-Transcendence."

7. Unamuno, *Tragic Sense*.

8. Wein, *Triumph of Survival*.

9. Heschel, *God in Search*, 193.

10. Berkowits, *Faith*.

during creation to make way for human free will. This put the entire universe into a metaphoric state of exile.[11]

Wiesel based his play *The Trial of God* on an experience he had in a concentration camp. Prisoners of every type—rabbis, scholars, factory workers, farmers—put God's character on trial. Addressing both covenantal and individual suffering, the jurors presented classical Jewish arguments across the spectrum.

One Job-like character, throwing up his hands in the face of God's inexplicable purposes, remembered his retort, "Have you commanded the morning since your days began, and caused the dawn to know its place?" (Job 38:12).

Though the free-will defense letting God off the hook seemed logically consistent to some, others complained that they had no responsibility for Adam's sin. Any fall from grace made God into a cosmic sadist who rigged the game from the start.

Ultimately, they judged God's character guilty. After the pronouncement came, one of the leaders turned to the group and asked, "What do we do now?" Succinctly and in unison, they all said, "Now, we pray."[12]

Would God would prefer this sort of agonized fidelity to ignoring him out of hand?

After reading this, I realized that I could never find comfort in praying to a completely alien deity.

11. Heschel, *God in Search*, 193.
12. Wiesel, *Trial of God*, 54.

CHAPTER 14

Jesus as Divine Pathos Personified

WITH SOME MIDDLING RESEARCH under my belt, I turned again to Yancey's *Where is God When It Hurts*? This time, my brain shifted, and I saw how the Jewish concepts of divine pathos, God's hiddenness, and vicarious suffering were tangibly represented on the cross of Jesus.

In *Night*, Wiesel concluded that the Almighty died on the gallows alongside the boy. In measures, I began to accept Yancey's contention—that God's living spirit stood in solidarity with the boy, sharing and identifying with his agony.

As to the question, "Where was God during the Holocaust?," Christians conclude that God is where he has always been—on the cross in complete identification with a suffering world. For me to assimilate this meant I had to separate the true meaning of the cross from the symbolism that had grown up around it in the Jewish mind. Pope John Paul II, formerly the bishop of Auschwitz, said in front of the crematoriums, "This is the Golgotha of our age."[1] With this jarring statement, he linked the cross to the torrid history of Jewish agony.

When I read about Jesus' last cry of forsakenness, I experienced a sense of discovery, as if coming to an unforeseen fork in the road leading to an alternate universe. I saw that what my mind couldn't conceive and that which my heart yearned for had resided with me all along. God, knowing my fallen nature, had granted me my capricious wish. When the Almighty hid his face for a time, Jesus, the God-man, experienced the ultimate psychic insult of separation from God.

Knowing that Jesus, divine pathos personified, identified with my spiritual alienation took the sting out of my own pain. I had only to abide with him on the cross without striving for hope or proper sacred feelings.

1. "Homily of His Holiness."

As I surrendered and identified with him in this way, hope asserted itself of its own accord. I revisit this meditative formula every time I need to rewire my spiritual synapses.

In *Pillar of Fire*, Stern, regarding the individuality of pain, quoted the opening lines of Anna Karenina: "All happy families are alike; each unhappy family is unhappy in its own way."[2] Remembering the ego-defining, unique benefits of shared pain, I reasoned, "How much more and to what better end would it be for me to share my singular affliction within the triune Godhead itself?" Communing with the trinity afforded me an infinite support group—Father, Son, and Holy Spirit relating to one another in mysterious transcendence.

2. Stern, *Pillar of Fire*, 263.

CHAPTER 15

Concepts of Atonement in Judaism and Christianity

MY SECOND REVELATION CENTERED on guilt. Though our family attended services on Yom Kippur, the Day of Atonement, in my righteousness I may have suspected that the liturgy applied to others and not to me. In *Mere Christianity,* C. S. Lewis wrote about those with natural geniality who have no recognition of their sin. In describing a righteousness known only to God, he concluded that some are so placed in this world that the sin of gossip ranks higher than the sin of murder.[1] This dreadful thought shifted the problem from the likes of Osama Bin Laden and Hitler to garden-variety sinners like me.

As a teenager, I lied to Mom to get around her excessive control. I continued this pattern into adulthood, even when unnecessary. A humorous event in my twenties illustrates my vanity.

Sashaying into the lobby of Manhattan's posh Plaza Hotel, I wore my new Ellen Tracy pantsuit and a paisley scarf tied around my neck. I sat in the tearoom next to the elegant clientele, where I drank champagne and ate petit-fours for nearly an hour. After paying the bill, I stopped in the ladies' room.

Outside, I sauntered down several well-populated blocks smug at the attention from men and women who glanced in my direction. At a corner, a woman kindly pointed to something amiss. A foot-and-a-half of silky white paper flowed from the back of my waist. I hadn't properly disengaged from the toilet paper after using the toilet. Mortified I learned to never again assume I looked good until first checking my grooming. What's more, I recognized I had a problem.

---

1. Lewis, *Mere Christianity*, 91.

The ultimate question for any of us, looking back, is, "How could I possibly have done that?" My most appalling sin began as a subtle habit. Like most sins of omission, it caught me unaware. The steamrolling, full-fledged consequence of my actions would soon bring me to my knees.

In trying to feign a cheerful attitude around Michael, I compartmentalized my pain, thinking it would help both of us. In moving away from co-dependency, however, I veered in the opposite direction. When his condition overwhelmed me, I froze my feelings, preferring to dissociate than have the breath sucked out of me. My heart, a warehouse of dusty memory, simply closed up shop.

Steve noticed the damaging effect my behavior had on Michael. What flaw in my personality caused me to vacillate from one extreme to the other? I couldn't get around, beyond, or past my execrable failure. With no excuse to soften the blow, I face the oppressive pangs of legitimate remorse.

I had tortuous memories of Michael, at nine, crying himself to sleep without being comforted by me. He has told me that he felt abandoned and totally alone in the universe. I'm told that children ignored in this way have greater problems than those who suffer physical abuse from a parent. My conscience stricken, I longed to stop the clock and rewind time. I had no way of undoing the damage I had done.

Given that repentance originated in Judaism, it puzzled me that I found so little in the current literature on the Jewish experience of conversion. Aside from examples in the Tanakh, my only way to compare the two modes of atonement was through experience and research. Despite believing that an all-powerful God can forgive whomever and wherever he chooses, I became convinced that Christianity affords greater power for forgiveness than Judaism.

My time of guilt coincided with Yom Kippur. Sitting with Mom in synagogue, I savored the readings. My blemished soul was stirred to the depths by the cadence of the cantor's chanting of Psalm 51, the pre-eminent prayer of repentance in Judaism. Scholars believe King David composed this after committing adultery with Bathsheba. Though I experienced penitential longing, the outcome was no more than a halfway house, transient and unsatisfying.

Only when I threw myself at the foot of the cross did my soul become substantially and permanently elevated. With every move I made toward Jesus, I felt his spirit cleaning every bit of muck and grime from my being. Divine love absolved my wrenching failure, and at last I found peace.

True to my nature, I wanted to analyze this mysterious alchemy. Psychologists distinguish between two types of love: unconditional mother love and conditional father love. God shows conditional love when he forgives after a change in behavior. He shows grace, or mother love, by offering forgiveness before a change occurs.

Because we need an impetus to get out of the cycle of sin, acceptance and forgiveness must come first. Grace, or undeserved forgiveness, is like getting a grade of an A from the outset: it erases the sting of fear and punishment. Naturally, I wondered whether this would lead to laziness or moral looseness. I learned, however, that real and rightly understood, grace leads to a radically changed nature.

The grace aspects inherent in Judaism have served to offset its more legalistic phases and keep it alive. Consistent with the overall pattern of Jewish history, Jews please God out of gratitude for forgiveness. Miroslav Volf, founding director of the Yale Center for Faith and Culture, agreed with Heschel's view that God initiates forgiveness through grace but added: "Christians claim much more. God has gone to such lengths that the sins that weigh you down have already been taken away."[2]

Regarding the mechanics of atonement, Christian psychiatrist Paul Tournier observed that primitive Indians, far removed in time and place from Old Testament rituals, recognized the need for animal sacrifice to attain closeness to a higher power.[3] A curious modern-day practice confirms this inherent psychological need. Before Yom Kippur, Orthodox Jews perform a ritual sacrifice called *Kaporos*. Men hold roosters, women hens as they pass the birds over their heads and say three times, "This is my substitute, this is my exchange, this is my atonement. This fowl will go to death, and I will enter upon a good, long life and peace."

Because the temple no longer exists, the Talmud states that Jews can obtain forgiveness through repentance, prayer, and performing good deeds. This told me that Christianity stresses God's outreach to man, and that Judaism stresses man's attempt to save himself.

When my all-consuming wretchedness prevented me from initiating reconciliation, God himself accomplished the work. The action is not only a theory about God but also an identification with the suffering and atoning work of Jesus. I could see that the cross, representing rarified grace and God's once-and-for-all atonement, gave Christianity its unique power.

2. Frymer-Kensky, *Christianity*, 317.
3. Tournier, *Guilt and Grace*, 174–80.

Because Judaism starts with the worth of humankind and the inherent goodness of creation, many see the Christian view as pessimistic. However, Blaise Pascal noted that Christianity teaches neither blind optimism nor resigned cynicism. He wrote, "Knowledge of God without knowledge of man's wretchedness leads to pride. Knowledge of man's wretchedness without knowledge of God leads to despair. Knowledge of Jesus Christ is the middle course, because by it we discover both God and our wretched state."[4]

James Bernstein, a Jew who converted to the Greek Orthodox faith, has contrasted the Eastern view of forgiveness with that of the Western Protestant church. In *Surprised by Christ,* he wrote that Protestants conceive of atonement in terms that imply pardon, debt, payment, and ransom. When the Orthodox read that Christ died for our sins, they understand it to mean that Christ died to heal us, to change us, and to make us more Godlike. He didn't die instead of us in the sense of paying a debt.[5]

The sacredness of the blood and its efficacy consists not in how the offering changes God but in how it changes the person offering it. Expiation is directed to that part of us that prevents perfect worship. Propitiation, on the other hand, implies transference of sin to the substitute seeking to appease God's offended will. Salvation, more than escaping death or hell, reflects the root meaning of health.

---

4. Zondervan, *1001 Quotations,* 696.
5. Bernstein, *Surprised by Christ.*

CHAPTER 16

Grueling Choices

Resistance obstructs movement only from a lower sphere to a higher. It kicks in when we seek to pursue a calling in the arts, launch an innovative enterprise, or evolve to a higher station morally, ethically, or spiritually.

—Steven Pressfield, *The War of Art*[1]

IF MICHAEL AND STEVE noticed the anxiety that almost sank me, they didn't acknowledge it. Now in seventh grade, Michael had his own problems—contending with after-school detention and ongoing preparations for his bar mitzvah.

After two epiphanies, the floodgates had opened for a titanic struggle. To trust in God's leading entailed the risk of being lost in translation in a community that I loved. I simply couldn't sync my new faith with the ambiguities of my life. The thread of Jewishness resided in my consciousness as a state of being, not a theoretical fact.

Warring forces caused a curtain of doubt and indecision to descend. I longed for closure but felt trapped between two worlds. Every half-grasped confirmation disintegrated into thin air, leaving me in a negative space like the push-pull between dueling magnets.

In my quandary, I turned to books exploring the mystery of Jewish survival and the nature of Jewish belonging. Many define Judaism in terms of religion, nationality, and political loyalty—the whole being more than the sum of its parts. Some suggest that the survival of our people proves the existence of God.

When Einstein presented an early paper on his theory of relativity, he stated that if he was proven correct, every country would claim him. If

---

1. Pressfield, *War of Art*, 16.

proven wrong, he said, "the French will call me Swiss, the Swiss will call me German, and the Germans will call me a Jew."[2]

I learned that *The Wizard of Oz* song "Somewhere Over the Rainbow" reflected the Jewish immigrant consciousness. Harold Arlen and Yip Harburg, who wrote the melody and lyrics, reached deep into their roots to express their idealistic hope for Jewish survival.[3]

Shapiro, in his article "The Rise of Secular Judaism," described the limits of Jewish identity. In the eyes of the Jewish community, converting to Christianity removes one from the fold, at least socially. He quotes Heinrich Heine's ironic quip, "No Jew can possibly become a Christian because a Jew could never believe another Jew could be God."[4]

Jewish law considers one who converts to another religion a sinner or heretic, but essentially a Jew. In their book *Boundaries of Jewish Identity*, Susan Glenn and Naomi Sokoloff claim that Jews themselves have a convoluted, complex dialog about how to define Jewishness. In modern Judaism, the boundaries of belonging have shifted because of multicultural and global changes.[5]

Shulamit Magnus, in her essay "Good Bad Jews," wrote of two Jewish Christians who challenged the lines between apostasy and loyalty in nineteenth-century Russia.[6] The converts, Daniel Chwolson and Lev Kupernik, earned the paradoxical status of "good bad Jews" because of their loyalty and work on behalf of Jewish causes.

Chwolson, a child prodigy and student of rabbinic literature, taught himself Latin and the rudiments of German, Russian, and French from dictionaries. He fled on foot to Breslau, Germany, where he studied classical and modern European languages. After completing his doctorate, he returned to St. Petersburg to become the chair of Oriental studies in Hebrew, Syriac, and Chaldaic philology.

Chwolson came to the attention of Nicolas I, who appointed him to a position at the Russian Orthodox Seminary. Chwolson earned the adoration of the Jewish community for vehemently denying any basis for the blood libel—the charge that Jews used Christian blood in religious ceremonies.

2. "Einstein on Classifications."
3. Shapiro, "'Over the Rainbow.'"
4. Shapiro, "Decline and Rise."
5. Glenn and Sokoloff, *Boundaries*.
6. Magnus, "Good Bad Jews."

Following the vindication of the Jews, the community escorted Chwolson to the synagogue. As they opened the Torah scrolls, an act reserved only for sacred liturgical moments, rabbis and scholars expressed their love and respect. No Jewish authority could have accomplished as much as he did.

Lev Kupernik, a brilliant unconventional rogue with a passion for justice, studied law at Moscow University. After falling in love with the daughter of an important justice official, he converted to Russian orthodoxy. He moved to Kiev, where he gained a reputation as a brilliant defense attorney and wandering dispenser of justice. Kupernik wrote editorials and articles attacking anti-Semitism and continued his association with Jewish friends and colleagues.[7]

I benefitted from reading memoirs by Jewish Christians—*Life in a Jewish Family*, by Edith Stein; *Pillar of Fire*, by Karl Stern; and *The Promise*, by Jean Marie Lustiger. Lustiger, a French cardinal in the Roman Catholic Church, had Jewish Ashkenazic roots. As a preteen, he came across a Protestant Bible and felt inexplicably attracted to it. As a thirteen-year-old, he converted to Roman Catholicism during Holy Week.[8]

In October 1940, the Vichy regime in France passed its first statute against the Jews, forcing them to wear a yellow Star of David badge. The Nazis deported Lustiger's mother to Auschwitz-Birkenau, where she died the following year. After this, Lustiger's father, seeking the help of the chief rabbi of Paris, tried to have his son's baptism annulled.[9]

Stein, a German Jewish philosopher who converted to Catholicism, became a martyr and a saint. Born into an observant Jewish family, her horror at the tragedies of World War I motivated her to become a nurse's assistant. Under the guidance of the philosopher Edmund Husserl, she completed her doctoral thesis and obtained an assistantship at the University of Freiburg.

Reading the works of St. Teresa, Stein was drawn to Catholicism. She and her sister, also a convert, went to a Carmelite monastery in the Netherlands. The Nazis arrested them in 1942 and sent them to Auschwitz, where they died in the gas chambers.[10]

Stern was born to socially assimilated parents, and, despite his sparse Jewish education, he eventually joined an Orthodox synagogue. A specialist

7. Magnus, "Good Bad Jews."
8. Lustiger, *Promise*.
9. Lustiger, *Promise*.
10. Stein, *Life*.

in psychiatric research, he emigrated from Nazi Germany to Canada. His encounters with such luminaries as Jacques Maritain and Dorothy Day led to a period of soul searching, after which he received baptism into the Catholic Church.[11]

It was during this period of reading that I attended two events in the Jewish community that helped clarify my thinking. At a fundraiser, I heard the speaker recount the long history of Jew-hatred, and I found myself thinking, "We Jews must certainly be more virtuous than others to have suffered so." Checking this impulse, I countered it with the idea that God himself has preserved the Jewish people.

Philip Gourevitch called the downside of this faulty view "easy righteousness." In the Jewish weekly the *Forward*, he warned about the common societal problem in which minorities value themselves according to their victimization.[12]

Several months later, I attended an annual Yom HaShoah service commemorating the six million who perished in the Holocaust. The full name of the day—*Yom HaShoah Ve-Hagevurah*—translates as Day of Remembrance of the Holocaust and the Heroism.

A large crowd gathered at Tree of Life temple to hear Moffatt Burris, a well-known war hero and concentration-camp liberator. Without the usual flowers and bright lights, the sanctuary looked somber. I talked briefly to my friend, Jason, who sat in the lobby nervously tuning his guitar.

As soon as the rabbi lit six large candles, oppressive guilt blindsided me. Pangs of conscience jammed my throat and caused my chest to tighten. I felt on my shoulders the weight of three thousand years of thought and memory. I had recently read Wiesel's contention that behind all anti-Semitism lies an unconscious strike against God. I wondered whether leaving Judaism would have the same unintended effect. In trying to pinpoint my guilt, I realized that I remained in the grip of the unconscious mantra of my environment: continuity as the be-all and end-all of Judaism. Intellectually, I had separated the cross from anti-Semitism, but emotionally I had not done so.

Not long afterward, I dreamed I was in a Polish concentration camp. Walking between the barracks, carefully avoiding refuse-filled pits, I glanced up at the ice-laden clouds. Dressed in threadbare clothing, I rubbed my hands together to stave off the bone-chilling cold.

---

11. Stern, *Pillar of Fire*.

12. Remnick, *Devil Problem*.

In the distance, I heard the call of a lone warbler. Looking for its source, I walked toward a patch of uninspiring birch trees several hundred feet away. As I approached, I could see a man peering up at the branches.

Moving closer, I noticed his dark, Semitic features, grief-stricken eyes, and stooped shoulders. After an agonizing moment, he turned to me and gazed with preternatural understanding. As if recognizing an old friend, he broke into an ebullient grin. His smile transformed his features and imbued his eyes with pure, limitless love.

Enraptured by his countenance, I began to move toward his outstretched arms, but stopped and gasped in shock. Raw, gaping wounds, red-hot and rancid, cut a wide swath in the palms of his hands.

When suddenly I awoke, my heart told me I had seen Jesus.

CHAPTER 17

Ultimate Surrender:
Being Loved to Death

When someone makes a decision, he is really diving into a strong current that will carry him to places he had never dreamed of when he made the decision.

—Paul Coelho, *The Alchemist*[1]

HAVING RESOLVED SUBSTANTIVE CONFLICT, I simply sat with myself, waiting for something to push me toward final surrender. In October, the local Catholic Church commemorated the twenty-second anniversary of "Nostra Aetate." The title of the Latin treatise, written by the Vatican in 1965, translates as "In Our Times." Focusing on the relationship between Jews and Catholics, it rejects the accusation of Jewish responsibility for Jesus' death—something used for centuries to justify persecution. It states, "What happened in his passion cannot be charged against all the Jews, without distinction, then alive, nor against the Jews of today."

Key members of the Jewish community took part in seminars focusing on reconciliation. I decided not to attend and went, instead, to the Sunday worship service.

Entering the sanctuary, I sat in the back next to a row of stained-glass windows. Morning light dispersed tinted rays across the pews. A red-and-gold bas-relief of the crucifix stood in the narthex; tall candles on either side cast shadows on the ceiling—to me they resembled minuscule dancing angels.

Father Doyle had craggy middle-aged features—crow's feet and ruddy, weather-beaten skin. His eyes had the winsome look of someone about to unveil a comic, mystical truth. He began by explaining how his

1. Coelho, *Alchemist*.

interaction with members of the Jewish community had caused him to ponder the key differences between the two faiths. He subsequently gave me a copy of his homily:

> In deep reverence and respect for our Jewish roots, I wish to elucidate ways in which Christianity takes faith a step further.
>
> Though Pinchas Lapide, an Orthodox Jewish New Testament scholar, attested to the truth of the resurrection, he never converted to Christianity. Lapide has implied that the habit of hope the Jews have mastered throughout the centuries is reflected in the resurrection. It provides a key to the mystery of the Jewish art of survival.[2]
>
> Last week, I read a passage by Amy Carmichael in *The Gold Cord*. A missionary in India, she wrote of a series of calamities that led to a time of great spiritual despondency. After the loss of a dear friend from cancer, she admitted that the burden had become too great for her. Sitting among the tamarind trees, she realized that they resembled the olive trees where Jesus knelt. She wrote, "And, I knew that this was His burden, not mine. It was He who was asking me to share it with Him, not I who was asking Him to share it with me. I could not help but kneel down beside Him under the olive trees."[3]
>
> I wish to explore the importance of what Jesus suffered in the Garden of Gethsemane. He agonized over God's will in his upcoming ordeal. Scripture recounts that His sweat fell like great drops of blood. Jurgen Moltmann, in *The Crucified God*, wrote, "God does not become a religion or a law merely for us to obey Him. When God became a man, He not only entered as a finite being but entered as one who experienced God-forsakenness."[4]
>
> Do you see why this is so important? God's indwelling spirit conforms to each soul, inhabiting the precise nature of a person's alienation. Every imaginable sorrow is subsumed under His last cry of forsakenness. This means that we can never sink so low in our spirit that Jesus has not gone deeper still. Our pain is but a drop in the bucket compared to his.
>
> Go now in peace and ponder what Jesus has done for you.

The service was a watershed for me. As I listened to the homily, every instance of life's injustices crystallized around Dad's recent diagnosis of Parkinson's disease. Tears streamed down my face, coming from a place

2. Lapide and Rahner, *Encountering Jesus*, 20.
3. Carmichael, *Gold Cord*, 31.
4. Moltmann, *Crucified God*, 414.

of such emptiness that I hadn't even known of its existence. Instead of my usual post-cry limpid state, I felt an infinite peace.

Looking at the bas-relief, I witnessed the transfiguration of divine suffering into love. With knowledge beyond reason, I realized that God's sovereignty encompassed and contained my every pain—past, present, or yet to come.

Having reached the ultimate place God had prepared for me, I would never again look back. The truth of Jesus' love, more important than anything I would be giving up, penetrated me with electric force.

Over the next week, Michael and Steve commented on my energy and contentment. Floating serenely above all mundane distractions, I stayed up late going deeper and deeper as I wrote in my journal. I reread a section of Peter Berger's *The Question of Faith* in which he recounted a dialogue from Dostoyevsky's *The Brothers Karamazov*. It took place between Alyosha and his non-believing brother, Ivan.

Ivan describes the punishment of a young boy who accidentally killed his master's favorite hunting dog. They forced the mother to watch as the boy stripped and ran from a pack of dogs who subsequently tore him to pieces. Alyosha asks Ivan what punishment the landlord deserves. Ivan basically says that even hell would not suffice and that, because there could be no force in the universe with the right to forgive, he would rather the boy stay unavenged and he unsatisfied.

Explicating the Christian response, Berger explained that God understands and endorses Ivan's anger, however misdirected. Though we will never understand why God permits Satan to initiate evil, through a process akin to kenosis God enters our pain and inaugurates the healing of our fallen planet. The love shown on the cross and the power of the resurrection finally reconcile these two aspects of God's nature. Each person in the episode will have a destiny beyond this life. Both the child and the mother will find infinite comfort, and the perpetrator, if unrepentant, will face God's judgment.[5]

At one time, I could only relate to the rebellious Ivan. Now, embracing the Christian worldview, I could place my motherly pain onto the shoulders of Jesus. With every actor in the divine scenario working for my healing, I came to identify with Mary, who witnessed her son's agony.

5. Berger, *Questions of Faith.*

The following afternoon, I hadn't done any housework or even begun to think about supper. I heard Michael and his friend Edmund playing in the backyard when Steve called to say he was on his way home.

When I walked into the bedroom, I saw clothes strewn in every direction. Making the bed, I became aware of my childlike affection for Jesus. I hoped that he, in turn, would understand every aspect of my serious, funny personality. This flash of whimsy served as a mellow counterpoint to the intense nature of my search.

Letting the barrier of time slip away, I put my chores aside and sat on a low stool near the closet. With Isaac Stern playing on the radio and the warmth of the setting sun on my back, I called upon every guileless, simple-hearted emotion in my nature and prayed:

> Jesus, today, I surrender every aspect of my being to you. Come into my life and overwhelm me with your spirit. I embrace you as my Lord and Savior and give you every measure of my devotion from everlasting to everlasting. Please forgive my sins and help me to become a better person. I'm sorry you had to go through so much in proving yourself to me. I am yours forever. And as fair warning, I am high maintenance.

CHAPTER 18

Shaking the Family Foundations

DESPITE HAVING QUESTIONS THAT still perplexed me, I had made an informal resolution. If I had waited for clarification on every point, I would never have begun the commitment phase of my journey. Besides, any issues troubling me paled in comparison to the real-world conundrums I was encountering with my loved ones.

It both shocked and dismayed me that the three I was closest to—Steve, Mom, and Dad—had the most difficulty with my faith. The more intense the bond, the greater was their sense of disorientation and betrayal. They didn't see it coming. They knew only one facet of my personality—the familiar, verifiable, and taken-for-granted side. No one should ever presume to know a person through and through, especially a loved one.

To their credit, they knew that I hadn't merely adopted a new set of beliefs but that I'd had a dramatic encounter with the person of Jesus. A mystifying, unknowable force had changed all the rules, trampling their bedrock sense of reality and eroding every notion of what they could conceivably control in life. It would take years before any of them could admit to my faith having any beneficial effect on me.

I revealed myself to Steve at the outset of a routine evening at home. By its end, an impenetrable variance had materialized out of thin air. We were both reading in bed when I looked up to survey walls in desperate need of repair. A jagged piece of sheetrock with samplings of blue stood facing us. Peering at it, I said, "Honey, let's go with the azure, in the middle. What do you think?"

Half listening, he said, "I'm not sure yet."

I blurted out, "Steve, I need to talk to you about something important. I need your attention, so let me know when you finish reading that."

Putting his book down, he said, "I'm done. I hope I haven't done anything wrong. Whatever it is, I'm apologizing for it in advance, OK?"

"No," I said, "It's nothing like that." I cleared my throat and added softly, "but it's very personal and you may not like it. It has to do with my Holocaust study and where it's led me."

With eyes widening, he said, "Gail, I'm glad Judaism has helped you, but I hope you're not going to say you want to live in Israel. I promise we'll go next year so please be patient."

"No, Steve," I said. "It's not that."

Looking me in the eye, he asked, "Do you want to become Orthodox? That would be an adjustment, but I can accept anything."

"No," I said. "It's not that."

"Then for God's sake, tell me, but just don't say you're having an affair with the rabbi."

"No, of course not." I forced a laugh.

He said, "Well, then, what the hell is it? Go ahead and spill the beans."

Wishing I'd never broached the subject, I thought of every way I could reverse course and not tell him. I said, "Just remember you said you could accept anything. Well, um . . . I don't know any other way to say it, but the fact is I believe what Christians believe. It's given me a lot of peace, and I'm convinced there's a strong intellectual basis for it."

His face turned red, and he began to shake. He said, "Well, that's one damn thing that I can never accept. Can you imagine what the Jewish community will do to you? They'll outright crucify you."

"Don't worry, Steve," I said. "I'm nowhere near talking about this."

Angrily, he retorted, "I don't know how any intelligent person could actually believe this crap. You stand behind the whole ball of wax, miracles and all?"

I said, "Well, I've never seen one, but I'm open to the possibility. I've read evidence in cosmology that proves the Big Bang, and prominent scientists believe that a supreme intelligence is behind the laws of the universe. If God wanted to intervene, he could. Steve, think about the things you might be willing to die for that you can't prove on paper. Would you just look at some of what I've been reading?"

He blurted out, "Well, as a matter of fact, I wouldn't, and I hope it's not a deal-breaker. Our marriage worked because neither of us was religious. I married a Jewish girl. What in the world has happened to you?"

I said gently, "Steve, I know, and I'll always feel Jewish."

Exasperated, he asked, "Just look at everything that comes down in this world. What kind of God would allow it?"

"Steve, I had the very same questions. I'm the one who studied the Holocaust. I hated God at one point, and it drove me to read more."

"Gail, Christians are the meanest, most narrow-minded devils I know."

Lowering my voice to almost a whisper, I said, "Steve, you're absolutely right. Some of them are, but God's not mean. Just trust me."

"I hope you're not going to say that I'm going to hell."

"Of course not," I said. "I'm not like that. The fact is, Steven—and I don't mean to sound snide—you wouldn't even enjoy heaven because you wouldn't be in charge. Admit it, you have a problem with control. Sometimes I feel like I married my mom."

"Listen," he said, "At some point, a person either decides to believe or not. Trust me, I'll never take that leap, so don't get your hopes up."

"Steve, don't use the whole leap thing as an excuse. You won't even look at the evidence. When I studied, it wasn't a leap at all—just a small step."

I wanted to smack the smirk clear off his face, but I managed to keep the atmosphere friendly as we readied for bed. I turned off the lights and tunneled under the covers, trying to fathom exactly how a few words about something eternal could unsettle such a mundane day.

That night, I had a jarring dream about a cataclysmic earthquake halfway around the world. Everything lay in shambles. When I awoke, I determined not to let our differences fissure the ground closer at hand.

Late, on the following afternoon, I called Mom saying, "I need to talk to you and Dad about something important. Can I come over?"

She said, "Of course, honey. Is everything okay?"

"Yeah, everything is fine. I'll be over in a flash."

The short distance up their familiar circular drive seemed endless and foreboding. I tried to calm my nerves by focusing on the yard—a delicate array of pink azaleas and throngs of butterflies chasing robins in flight. Mom and I had named this time of day "magic hour" because of the dwindling, shimmery light. Remembering such ultimate realities as truth, justice, and beauty, I muttered a short prayer and stepped up the stoop to ring the doorbell.

The three of us sat in the sunroom with a view to the pool and the lake beyond. In the distance, dismal cloud formations warned of yet another late-night thunderstorm. A series of them had besieged the area for more than a week

My voice shaking, I said, "You're not going to like what I'm about to say, but I have to tell you. I've kept it secret for too long."

Dad turned pale and began to fidget. Mom swallowed hard, her eyes darting nervously.

I said, "Well, you both know about my Holocaust study and how I've become a more spiritual Jew. It helped me for a while, but our problems with Michael—and I haven't told you everything—have caused me to delve deeper.

"For the last year, I have been veering toward Christianity. It's given me tremendous sustenance, and, for the first time, in years, I feel fully alive." Looking at their faces, entombed now in ancient sorrow, I realized they would have preferred me to say that I was getting a divorce, or had become a Republican.

I said, "Look at me, Mom. I'm a Jew. Jesus was a Jew. I will always cherish my roots and the values you and Dad have given me. They make me who I am today."

Dad said, "Have you gone down this road alone or are you involved with some kind of cult like Jews for Jesus? I've heard they prey on Jews who're uninformed."

I said, "Totally alone, Dad, and I'm not uninformed. I can put my knowledge of Judaism up against anything you and Mom have. But even if I studied Judaism for a lifetime, it could never resolve suffering in the way Christianity has."

Dad said, "Does this mean you actually believe in miracles?"

"Steve asked the same thing," I said. "Yes. But that doesn't make me a raving lunatic."

He asked, "Would you be willing to study with Rabbi Epstein?" This was the Orthodox rabbi in Columbia associated with the Chabad-Lubavitch movement in Brooklyn, New York. That my secular parents could relate to his charismatic nonjudgmental outreach spoke volumes. They considered him a close family friend.

I said, "I'd love to. I'm hungry for conversation. By the way, Dad, you may not realize it, but he believes in miracles, too."

Dad didn't answer.

Trying to engage Mom, I said, "Do you remember the day I asked you whether you thought God loves us as much as we love our children? You said, 'No, I don't think he could possibly take on that much pain.' Well, I've learned that he does, Mom, and it's turned my life around."

Dad, looking pensive, asked, "Gail, what about Christian anti-Semitism? We've suffered hatred for centuries. How in God's name can you reconcile that?"

"Dad, it's a great question and one that I've agonized over. I'll never be able to reconcile it. If I do, I'll get back to you."

"And, Gail," he said, "I don't want you to take this the wrong way, but you've suffered from prejudice yourself. None of us can forget those phone calls when you were in middle school. I just want you to honestly consider something. Is there a part of you that wants to cozy up to the enemy?"

"Dad, I feel more Jewish than ever. It's not the church or other Christians that I identify with. Besides, the rejection I've felt connects me more to Jesus. You should know me better than to think this is about joining some snobby social club.

"I've looked at this from every angle, and it just doesn't work to use unconscious motives to explain belief. I could use the same logic to explain why you're still an atheist. You can poke holes in someone's belief, but you can't ever fully explain it away."

Mom asked, "What does Steve say about this?"

"Well, I told him last night. I'm sure he's still in a state of shock. As you know, he's an agnostic."

We talked until the sun dimmed. "Before I leave," I said, "I want to tell you both how much I love you, and I'll be here for you as you work through this."

Mom uttered the only untruth spoken when she said, "Gail, I don't understand, but I'll listen because I want to understand."

Though I predicted Mom's strong reaction, the level of toxic emotions that later surfaced shocked me. The issues raised, though not religious as such, touched on control, loyalty, and cultural identity—all with deep, primal significance. Though Dad remained detached, Mom grieved. Later, she described her initial shock and denial, then the pain of losing someone she hardly recognized anymore. She wondered what she could have done wrong and looked for something or someone to blame.

Over the next year, Mom and I painstakingly worked through our difficulties. She held out the hope that my sessions with Rabbi Hesh Epstein would bring me around or, if that failed, surely her beloved son-in-law would prevail.

She may have intuited the unsettling half-truth that I had transitioned to a realm that didn't include her. I can compare this to what I felt years later, when she lay dying in hospice care. Seeing her disengage from this world in preparation for the next, I felt a combination of rage and sorrow—made all the worse because I couldn't direct it toward her. Through no fault of her own, she was deserting me.

Knowing of Mom's subsequent faith journey, I believe that she both envied and feared my faith. I had examined my doubts more seriously than she had examined hers. In spiritual parlance, she stood "under conviction" because of unconscious doubt.

Because Steve disbelieves as strongly as I believe, we both feel the separation. Though I've traveled a distance in his secular shoes, he has no way of understanding my point of view. When on the rare occasion we discuss religion, I become unable to articulate arguments I've long since resolved. As a one-time skeptic, I too easily identify with his viewpoint.

My words, even at their best, would likely fall on unhearing ears. Faith is an inside job, inaccessible through logic. An ineffable knowing exists among those of us who have been tapped on the shoulder and named by God. This chasm reflects not so much a communication problem as an experiential one. People with disparate worldviews often experience the world differently. As a result, there is little common ground for discussion. George Lakoff, a cognitive linguist, explored the concept of frames—deep-seated mental structures that determine how we view the world. Because of the way these paradigms play out, people can see the same set of facts and arrive at completely different conclusions.[1]

Steve has little interest in discussing anything that even touches on the sacred. Over the years, as the subject became taboo, I began to compartmentalize the deepest parts of me. Locked tight in an inner sanctum, they remained inaccessible to the very person I love the most—my husband.

After reading a short piece I'd written about my journey, a male friend said, "This is the sexiest thing I've ever read." I should have understood the dynamic. Steve knows that my bond with Jesus entails emotional intimacy with another man. One night at the kitchen table, he looked at me with searching eyes, and said, "At least in this world let me feel as though I'm your number one man."

With an awareness of the space every person needs for spiritual formation, I trust that the mystery and sincerity of my walk will penetrate as

1. Lakoff, "In Politics."

much from what is left unsaid as said. I'm also banking that my faith, lived out in contrast, will amplify in unique and provocative ways. If there is such a thing as spiritual resistance, my life embodies it.

To cage the elephant in the room, Steve and I often give voice to the spiritual loneliness that challenges our marriage. We reach over the void by building up other aspects of our relationship—ones permeated with their own timbre of sacredness. The intimacy, shared values, and mutual respect we have cultivated show that grace has worked its art in our forty-five-year marriage.

I can only hope that God understands agnostics like Steve—angry about life's injustice or simply angry at those who speak from the pulpit. I've noticed among many like Steve, a greater intellectual and emotional sensitivity than among certain Christians. For example, Steve cries to distraction every time he watches the musical *Les Miserables*. His tears betray him on cue at every scene depicting God's bewildering grace.

He also contends that Karl Malden, the priest in *On the Waterfront*, should have received an Oscar. He becomes emotionally charged every time he hears Father Barry's rousing speech depicting how a crucifixion occurs every time an honest worker is prevented from testifying against evil.

Though Steve may have valid criticisms of certain Christians, he mistakenly projects them onto God himself—shooting at the wrong target, like a straw man. Though some have suggested that the behavior of Christians constitutes the best argument against Christianity, I prefer instead Rabbi Heschel's contention that God is greater than religion.[2]

In classic conversion theory, a convert goes through enculturation, breaking ties to a former social network. Sociologists consider this a form of secondary socialization, because it gives new belief plausibility and allows it to take root.[3] Living in the same city as my parents, I couldn't follow a path even remotely similar to this, even if I desired it. Steve and I had benefitted from my family's many rich associations in Columbia, but I often longed for the anonymity that another community could have provided.

I mistakenly presumed that my belief would constitute just another one of my interests or hobbies. However, the clock had already begun ticking, and faith, once seen, cannot be watered down or turned back. Though many people of faith describe a sense of living in two worlds, my situation presented greater challenges. As a liberal Jew living in the Bible

2. Heschel, *Insecurity of Freedom*, 119.

3. Rambo, "Theories of Conversion."

Belt, I didn't exactly fit the mold of an evangelical believer. I knew that when I claimed Jesus openly and honestly, I would have to cross unnatural cultural boundaries.

My sister Laurie, who resides in Columbia, had a conversion experience several years after mine. Unlike my epiphany, hers mirrored the sudden born-again experience. She and her husband, Ken Walden, had recently moved from Upper Marlboro, Maryland, where they lived a rural life—cornfields, horse farms, and a flyway with hundreds of geese. Understandably, Laurie had difficulty adjusting to Columbia. Reconnecting with family caused some emotional upheaval, leading her to question her purpose in life. Tending toward New Age philosophy, she read a Christian book I had conspicuously left on my kitchen desk.

In the hospital recovering from minor surgery, she watched an episode of Pat Robertson's *The 700 Club* on TV and heard an interview with Christian writer Stormie Omartian. Laurie joined in the concluding prayer, then repeated it. She awoke the next morning filled with light, love, and calm. Later, she learned that several Christian acquaintances had been praying for her. Today, she maintains a close relationship with them in church, prayer group, and Bible study.

Laurie uses her writing skills as a legislative aide at the State House in Columbia. She has completed the master gardener course and the master naturalist course, becoming a talented photographer of rare birds. Talking about faith issues as they relate to family dynamics has helped both of us cope during a time of great flux. Her quintessential free spirit, humor, and open-hearted affection emboldens me and compels me to say, "She is my best friend."

CHAPTER 19

Hibernation Years

DURING THE NEXT FIFTEEN years, Michael's problems grew worse and with graver consequences. I kept my faith largely a private matter, but my relationship with Jesus kept me from descending into wholesale nervous collapse. Relying on him, I established a middle ground between co-dependence and disassociation.

After middle school, Michael attended Spring Valley High School and then Cardinal Newman High. These years brought a fresh round of irascible behavior and poor school performance. We considered sending him away to school but decided against it. Though for a time I pushed for it, part of me wanted him to stay home so I could make up for past mistakes.

Michael wrote:

In high school, I was bulimic. By the age of eighteen, it shifted toward anorexia. At nineteen, I tried drugs for the first time. Not until I was twenty-two, did I begin the daily habit of using drugs and alcohol to cope with my anorexia.

In four years at the University of Georgia, he completed only half of his requirements. In retrospect, I can see that we enabled him by allowing him to stay with minimal success. After UGA, he went to three treatment centers: the Medical University of South Carolina, in Charleston; Pavilion, in Asheville, North Carolina; and Pacific Hills, in Laguna Beach, California.

During these years, Steve and I faced harsh realities. Together, we mourned the future we envisioned for Michael. Because friends in our immediate circle had no experience with depression or drugs, we felt socially isolated. Absorbed with their own problems and concerns, they had no clue about the private devastation and unrelenting hell we endured.

Good friends didn't know whether to ask about Michael. In stilted conversations, they hesitated speaking of their own parental concerns, knowing they sounded trivial in comparison. If, as sociologists contend, Judaism is a child-centered culture, it explains why I had such difficulty attending cocktail parties in the community: no one wasted any time in recounting their children's successful milestones.

I found research backing up the statement, "You're only as happy as your unhappiest child." Researcher Karen Fingerman wrote about how problems with adult children can affect the well-being of their parents.[1] Though mothers bear the brunt, fathers often feel exhausted by ongoing uncertainty about their child's future. In *When Your Adult Child Breaks Your Heart*, Ann-Marie Ambert wrote that the desire for parental pride, hard-wired into our brains, reflects our instinctive desire for immortality.[2]

Though Steve and I are educated, resourceful people with the means to provide facilities and counseling, we had difficulty finding the proper care for Michael. For fifteen years, we relied on the advice of a therapist I will call Dr. M. Without revealing details of our therapy, in the middle of the process circumstances forced me to decide whether I should continue in his care or go elsewhere. After much prayer, I decided to stay. Years later, I could see that further counsel was a worthless squander of energy and resources. Though he doesn't bear blame for certain decisions we made, he bears blame for his advice about an important family dynamic. As it played out, it caused yet another layer of complication and pain.

Strategies and Lifestyle Changes

For years, my focus on obstacles and fears prevented me from appreciating what I had. By sheer force of will, I began practicing gratitude. As I cultivated the habit, it became second nature. I focused on such simple things as rubbing the sleep from my eyes without pain, the nape of Steve's neck, and then the act of gratitude itself. This new perspective made space for the contradictoriness of my experience. Even with a broken heart, I could have moments of profound fullness.

The Talmud, a book of Jewish commentary, describes Leah as the first woman in the Bible to practice gratitude. She spent years aching for the love of her husband, Jacob, repeatedly convincing herself that perhaps it

1. Young and Adamec, *When Your Adult Child*, 8.
2. Young and Adamec, *When Your Adult Child*, 6.

84

would come soon. Eventually she found the courage to accept that her life would not turn out as she had hoped. Rather than sinking into sorrow, she embraced the beauty and fullness of knowing that her four children would beget the entire nation of God's covenant.[3]

Despite my initial trepidation, I began to cultivate mindfulness through meditation. I learned that when my mind wandered, the simple act of reining it in improved brain function. This meant that, as with grace, I got an A from the start and couldn't go wrong. Visualizing my loved ones during meditation enabled me to combine it with intercessory prayer.

By worrying about the future and ruminating about the past, I had become a victim of my fulminations about time. Recognizing that Jesus is one with me as my life unfolds, I cultivated an awareness of every precious moment sanctified by God.

Because we can't hear, smell, or taste time, it has an illusory nature. Like the slow meandering of a river, we sense its passage only in relation to the changes on the bank. It expands or contracts based on our busyness. I considered such sayings as "a watched pot never boils" or "haste makes waste" and realized that expectancy causes time to slow down. If, as Shakespeare noted, "What's past is prologue," every present moment contains eternity. If time flies when we're having fun and grinds to a halt in the dentist's chair, I could make it stand still by savoring a moment of past rapture.

Philosophers have compared the Greek and Hebrew understanding of time. While the Greeks focused on its ephemeral, philosophical nature, they also valued its chronological aspects. The Hebrews, however, valued the qualitative aspects of the calendar. For example, Old Testament figures differentiated events not by their chronological position but by their spiritual impact.[4]

In her book *One Thousand Graces*, Ann Voskamp, reflecting on the Hebrew understanding, described *eucharisteo*, or giving thanks, as the process of slowing time and multiplying it.[5]

Several years into my commitment phase, I began the practice of journaling. Although rigorous and punishing, the exercise helped me overcome the psychic dissonance involved with my conversion. I could frame my story as a coherent whole by connecting my past, present, and future. I had moved away from theological Judaism, yet it remained the dominant

3. Palatnik, "Leah."

4. Branover and Ferber, "Concept of Absolute"; "Hebrew v. Greek."

5. Voskamp, *One Thousand Gifts*, 72.

narrative of my life. I will continue to align myself with an oppressed, marginalized culture because I want to witness, honor, and respect that part of me. My experience of anti-Semitism, for example, forged the character and resilience that defines me today.

I continue to write so that I can better know what I feel and think about a matter. As a form of communication that reaches deep into my psyche and speaks to a subconscious part of my soul, it resembles prayer. For example, as I looked out of my window on one recent morning, I noticed the difficulty of pinpointing the precise moment darkness turned to light. Only by putting pen to paper could I see that the stages of my life had been discerned this way—after the fact, and only subtly.

I grasped that my conversion evolved not from a single illumination but from many incremental points of light. My resistance to faith began to wear down when I began studying the Jewish roots of Christianity. By conceptualizing myself as a first-century Jewish believer, I could live in a world of my own understanding, apart from rigid cultural and religious stereotypes.

Yet the very act of recording memories and reflections caused me to second-guess myself. I wondered to what extent penning a memoir could signal that I was taking myself too seriously. I also wondered to what extent I should trust my early recollections.

After much thought, I concluded that it was just as likely I could take myself for granted as take myself too seriously. This realization led me to a finely tuned sense of wonder about all things routine—not only aspects of my life but stereotypic ideas about time, pain, and death that I had simply accepted.

In his *Reflections on the Psalms*, C. S. Lewis wrote about our surprise when we encounter something as ordinary as the passage of time. "We are so little reconciled to time that we are astonished at it. 'How he's grown!' we exclaim, 'How time flies!' as though the universal form of our experience were again and again a novelty."[6]

An imperceptible inbred awareness of our eternal nature causes the disparity and catches us off guard. I see the same dynamic at play when I hear that someone has suddenly died. I exclaim, "Why I just saw him, yesterday," as if that death couldn't possibly interrupt time.

Whether memory is a blessing or a curse, humans have a clearly defined knack for it. The meaning of our lives plays out in the trusted space

6. Lewis, *Reflections on Psalms*, 161.

between the truth known and the truth promised—often escaping us in the present only to be understood later. Alice, in Lewis Caroll's *Through the Looking Glass*, derided memory because it only worked backward.[7] Too bad she might say that hindsight only works to benefit the future.

The nineteenth-century French writer Marcel Proust predicted what modern neurology now confirms—that a long-ago memory is often a reconstruction of the past rather than a replay of it. Yet contrasting research suggests that a casual remembrance can have authentic, symbolic meaning in a person's long-term story.[8] As I became more mindful of my cumulative memories, I began to see them play out in reliable, coherent fashion.

Going back to a childhood home and seeing its reduced stature can produce an uncanny, unsettling effect. Because the universality of this trick implies a leveling of the playing field, I decided that should I continue to write I had no choice but to trust my memory.

Secret Alliances

I revealed my faith to only a select few during these years—in particular, Rabbi Epstein, a Chasid, and two very close Christian friends. On the afternoon that Rabbi Epstein visited, he said, "I'm honored that you have chosen me to tell your story. You can trust me." I studied with him for more than a year and continue to value his wisdom, depth of insight, and validation of my Jewishness. Because of him, I have grown to understand the grace aspects inherent in Hasidic Judaism and why Martin Buber described Christianity as the first Hasidic movement in Jewish history.[9]

Aside from our differences on certain social issues and the obvious one regarding Jesus, our approach reflects the same worldview. Our voices echo back and forth in a struggle of almost cosmic proportions. Although we remain at the center of the conflict, secular Jews and Christians stand only on the periphery, not touching or even understanding the boundaries that define our differences.

Our invigorating and thought-provoking discussions motivated me to learn more about his movement. The Chabad-Lubavitch sect arose as a spiritual revival in Western Ukraine during the eighteenth century. A reaction to the intellectualism in some branches of Judaism, it stresses exuberant

7. Carroll, *Through Looking Glass*.

8. Tukey, "Notes."

9. Friedman, *Martin Buber*.

and heartfelt prayer. Their messianism grounds itself in the works of the Zohar. Followers contend that they can hasten the coming of the Messiah, or *Moshiach*, by performing *mitzvot*, or good deeds.

Rabbi Menachem Mendel Schneerson, the last leader of the Chabad-Lubavitch movement, promoted worldwide outreach. Many of his followers believed that he was the long-awaited Messiah. After he died in 1994, leaders of the group, expecting his resurrection, made the decision not to replace him.

Shaul Magid, in his book *Hasidism Incarnate*, wrote that this group's controversial beliefs call upon Christian concepts such as the incarnation, the dual nature of God, and the divinity of the Messiah—why mainstream Jews consider them heretical.[10] Fascinated by the possibilities the scenario provided, I couldn't wait to hear Rabbi's Epstein's beliefs about Schneerson, known to his followers as the Rebbe.

Two years after Schneerson's passing, Rabbi Epstein and I met, as usual, at my parents' house. He wore a black-brimmed hat and a long jacket reminiscent of a bygone era. He had a slightly gray full beard and dark Semitic features—the best of them being eyes that dance with delight at the slightest hint of mirth.

We exchanged pleasantries and then sat at the dining-room table. After gathering my papers, I wasted no time in asking, "Rabbi, do you believe Schneerson was the Messiah?"

With raised eyebrows and a half-grin, he said, "I don't know. I defer to Maimonides here. As you know, Maimonides, probably the greatest Jewish thinker, lived in the twelfth century. He said that the messiah would have to meet certain requirements. Jews will have to come back to faith, there will be a physical ingathering in Israel, the temple will have to be rebuilt, and we will have peace on earth.

"After the Rebbe's death, only a vocal minority believed in his messiahship. The Rebbe himself discouraged such speculation. Maimonides said that the Messiah must be alive—if he dies, he's not the Messiah."

I asked, "So Judaism has no concept of the Messiah coming back?"

"Well, after he died, scholars searched the rabbinic literature. An obscure reference in the Talmud says that if the Messiah is from the land of the living he would be this rabbi or that rabbi, and if he's from the dead he would be the prophet Daniel."

I asked, "Do some believe that Schneerson was divine?"

10. Magid, *Hasidism Incarnate*.

He said, "No more divine than any of us. He had a deep connection with his divine soul, but each of us is made in the image of God."

Referring to my notes, I said, "Elliot Wolfson, who writes extensively on kabbalism, noted that long before the current controversy, Chabad pointed toward a divine, suffering Messiah. He contended that the Dead Sea Scrolls and other inter-testamental texts confirm this: The Self-Glorification Hymn has as its hero one whom God elevated above the angels.[11] This sounds like a direct forerunner of Jesus. I've read that rabbinic Judaism suppressed these views because the rabbis defined their beliefs in opposition to Christianity. After a long interval, these concepts returned and were written into the kabbalah.

"Raphael Patai confirms that the Tanya [the main work of Hasidic philosophy] identifies the Holy spirit, or *Shekinah*, as the second person in the Godhead."[12]

He said, "I don't know. That's a little above my pay grade. But in the sense that God becomes physical, I don't think it means that."

I said, "Rabbi, I know that Isaiah 53 is controversial. Some Christians believe that the suffering servant refers to Jesus and, of course, Judaism contends it references Israel. Do you have a problem with the fact that the Zohar gives it a messianic interpretation?"[13]

"I don't," he said. "Whether it refers to Israel or the coming Messiah, it doesn't really matter. Sometimes the Bible used them interchangeably because the Messiah also represented the nation."

I said, "I've read of a Jewish concept affirming that the death of the righteous serves as an atonement for the nation or the world. This sounds Christian."

The rabbi explained, "This doesn't mean that the death itself actually atones. It just means that when someone righteous dies, it motivates others around him to repent."

I countered, saying, "But Jacob Milgrom, in his *JPS Torah Commentary: Numbers*, wrote that Phineas's deed in sacrificing one human being assuaged God's wrath and thereby secured atonement."[14]

He said, "That's an interesting way of looking at it. I don't think I've ever heard that."

11. Wolfson, "Body in Text."
12. Patai, *Messiah Texts*, 182.
13. Wolfson, "Messianism."
14. Milgrom, *JPS Torah Commentary*.

In conclusion, I said, "Rabbi, you may not see it and, of course, I'd be happy to share my research, but I've found many parallels between mystical Judaism and Christianity. On some level, one might consider my views to be Jewish in origin. I feel that I've come full circle. Do you know of any secret Christians in Chabad?"

He laughed and said, "Well, if they're secret, I wouldn't know about them." After this humorous aside, his expression turned serious. "Gail, I certainly admire your quest. It's honest and authentic. It's easy to go along and accept what you've been taught, but you've sought out God on your own terms. It's a path of discovery, and only good things can come from it."

"Thank you, Rabbi. I remember the first time we met you indicated that if one of your children left Judaism you'd prefer for him to go my route than to be without God."

He said, "Yes. I can't imagine anything worse than that."

I continued, saying, "I recently read an article in *Hadassah* Magazine in which a rabbi confirmed that a family's beloved pet could be considered Jewish. I figure that if a dog can be Jewish and an atheist can be Jewish, so can I."

Softly, he offered, "Gail, you have a Jewish soul. No one can take that away from you."

The rabbi had to leave early to prepare for Shabbat. Mom and Dad joined came from the library to say hello, and the three of us saw him to the door. We then moved into the kitchen.

As the afternoon dimmed, Mom's expression turned from one of hesitancy to serious intent. As if led by some ancient impulse, Mom opened the cupboard and looked for an artifact seldom seen and seldom used in our house—a pair of Shabbat candlesticks inlaid with silver and gold.

Finding them, she lit the candles as we prayed: "Blessed are you, O Lord, our God, sovereign of the universe, who hallows us with mitzvot and commands us to kindle the Shabbat lights." We hadn't enjoyed the ritual since I was a child.

I put aside my tendency to stereotype people into rigid categories when two Christian friends on the other side of the cultural divide loved me out of my smug intolerance. I have prayed weekly for twenty-two years with Gaye Whitmire and Lillian Ginn. An experiment I presumed would have little chance of success has become one of the richest experiences of my life. Our sacred space, comprising laughter, tears, secrets, and accountability, remains the most serene part of my week. Lillian recently reminded me that for the first month I sat there, quietly crying and unable to join in.

Once, I told them, "I've gained far more than you because my problems were worse. I'm afraid I used you." Almost in unison, they responded, "We're happy to be used by God." I often picture Spike Lee documenting the clash of cultures as we bridge of our respective zip codes. I'm certain they never expected to encounter a sassy liberal Jew such as myself, and I confess to never expecting I would have such conservative friends.

The mere act of stepping into another's shoes and seeing the world through another's eyes keeps us humble. The mutual respect and intensity of our discussions call to mind Buber's I-Thou dialogue—the sacred manner in which he encountered God and his fellow man.

Our different views on the inerrancy of Scripture impact practically everything we discuss—salvation, end times, creationism, and social issues. Nevertheless, our commonality runs deeper than any of the issues that divide. Our agreement on the central tenets gives us the freedom to examine the margins that define our differences. Interspersed between bouts of nervous hilarity, we pray. We access a spiritual faculty that connects us on a deeper level—where the Almighty, alone, holds together contradiction and paradox.

I admit that in my liberal posture, I display far more judgment and dogmatism than they do. I respect their literal living out of the following passages:

> Love is patient and kind; love is not jealous or boastful; it is not arrogant or rude. Love does not insist on its own way; it is not irritable or resentful; it does not rejoice at wrong, but rejoices in the right. Love bears all things, believes all things, hopes all things, endures all things (1 Cor 13:4–7).

> A new commandment I give to you, that you love one another; even as I have loved you, that you also love one another. By this all men will know that you are my disciples, if you have love for one another (John 13:34–35).

> Judge not, that you be not judged. For with the judgment you pronounce you will be judged, and the measure you give will be the measure you get. Why do you see the speck that is in your brother's eye, but do not notice the log that is in your own eye? (Matt 7:1–3).

The passion Gaye and Lillian have for intercessory prayer has opened me up to God in ways I had been blind to. The irony is that at times we may pray at cross-purposes—I, that they will become less literal in their exegesis; they, that I will become more so.

After years of impassioned pleas, four people for whom we prayed became followers of Jesus. I've heard it said that God gives immediate answers to newcomers to the fold—the assumption being that seasoned Christians can better handle the wait. Whether or not this is true, I can state that the arduous path of developing patience has given me appreciation for the often-repeated phrase in the Hebrew Scriptures, "It came to pass."

We often relate stories about serendipitous events—the confluence of the extraordinary with the ordinary—that we call miracles. Some we have witnessed ourselves, some we have read about, and some have been passed on to us. Despite my incredulous tendency, I have no hesitation in confirming veracity to the stories below.

In *Bruschko and the Motilone Miracle,* Bruce Olson wrote about his twenty-eight-year mission with the Motilone Indians in the South American jungles.[15] Marxist guerrillas captured him and kept him in a prison camp where they tortured him psychologically and physically. After suffering from malaria, Olson had a severe attack of diverticulitis, causing him to lose more than two quarts of blood.

In agony and longing for death, he heard a melody from a songbird called a mirla. Olson, drifting in and out of consciousness, believed that the mirla sang for him. The haunting call brought to his mind Christ's resurrection. As light from the full moon poured through the jungle canopy, Olson felt the call's restorative effect on his soul and found himself coming back to life with every note. He realized that the bird was mimicking the familiar minor key chords that he and his former missionary brothers sang in their worship services.

Olsen believed that the greatest victory of his captivity was not his release but the song of the mirla in the moonlight. He never lost sight of God's sovereignty in orchestrating his circumstances in tandem with his brothers.

Another story centers on a man named Ken, who was serving a life sentence in a prison outside Columbia, South Carolina. After Ken escaped, a guard named John found him in a swampy area several miles away. A chase ensued. When John had him in his sights, something remarkable happened.

---

15. Olson and Lund, *Bruchko.*

Though not a religious man, John sensed God's direction not to shoot him. Years passed, and John completely forgot about the episode.

Back in prison, Ken had an astonishing conversion experience in which he turned his life over to Christ. He began teaching the Bible and won over many of his fellow-inmates. After ten years of exemplary behavior, he was released. He found a job in Columbia, where he led Bible study at a church he had recently joined.

A recently divorced man who had fallen on hard times happened to join Ken's Bible study. On the first day of class, he recognized Ken as the man he almost killed years ago. The two men exchanged memories of that fateful day, and John dedicated his life to Christ under Ken's tutelage.[16]

One morning, in Charleston, eager to get back to Columbia, I got dressed in a hurry. Without my glasses on, I mistakenly took two medicines that shouldn't have been combined. I got into my car, adjusted the mirrors, and started driving toward the highway. I saw the tall streetlamps on either side of King Street before falling into a semi-conscious state. I swerved into oncoming traffic before a patrolman pulled me over. He took me to the emergency room where they pumped my stomach out and discovered the problem. At the precise time I was in danger, Lillian, sensing my need, got down on her knees and prayed.

Every morning, Lillian calls out the names of her grandchildren and asks God to protect them. One morning, though questioning the tediousness of the task, she prayed as usual. Later in the day, her daughter-in-law, Bryn, walked out of a Walmart in Texas, her three children in tow. Brett, only four at the time, ran ahead of her into the path of a moving car. Unable to grab him, she screamed and ran toward him. Finally, she said, "Brett, I thought that car hit you."

Brett said, "No, Mom. It almost did, but you pulled me by my shirt out of the way." Lillian, assuming angels at work, never questioned the routine again.

A good friend holding to a conservative view of salvation feared that her recently deceased mother-in-law had not accepted Jesus before death. During the time she prayed for reassurance, she read about several nurses at a local hospital who found an abandoned infant they named Baby Grace. The newspaper article gave the exact location where the nurses found the child—underneath the funeral topiary at the mother-in-law's gravesite.

16. Olson and Lund, *Bruchko.*

Gaye, Lillian, and I pray in my sunroom, which affords a view of an assortment of birds. Once, seeing a particularly beautiful one, I exclaimed, "Oh, look! I think it's a painted bunting." I grabbed the binoculars so Gaye and Lillian could get a closer look.

Gaye waxed, "I've never in my life seen so many vivid colors on one bird. The greens and blues are so sharp and just look at that canary yellow! Today, God has given us a splendid display of his glory through nature."

I often wished that some of Gaye's grandiose enthusiasms for God would rub off on me. When the flutter of commotion settled down, we prayed for family and friends for almost an hour.

Never afraid of controversy, I brought up the thorny question of Israel by asking, "Did you see the piece on CNN last night criticizing Obama's treatment of Israel?"

Gaye said, "No, but I can only imagine. Obama has sold Israel down the river."

I said, "Well, as you know, I'm somewhere in the middle here. Like many in Israel, I often question the settlements, but I'm far from believing Israel is an apartheid state."

Gaye, in a kind but firm tone, said, "Gail, you need to read what the Bible says about the end times. The prophecies say that for Jesus to come back, the Jews must return to the land. It's happening right before our eyes, and we need to support Israel in every that way we can."

Politely, I said, "Gaye, many respected evangelicals have come to believe that the prophecies on Israel were fulfilled non-literally through Jesus."[17]

Lillian said, "Gail, I'm with Gaye. I think you should read what the Bible says about it."

"But, Lillian, it's not what the Bible *says*, it's what the Bible *means*. Complicated views on either side tell me to be discerning."

Lillian countered, "But, Gail, how can you even begin to discern if you leave out the Bible?" For a minute, Lillian caught me off guard. I said, "Lillian, you have a good point there."

Lillian said, "Well, prophecy is just another one of those differences we have to die to." This was her expression for surrendering to God. "Gail, why don't you lead us in prayer for the peace of Jerusalem?"

Never were there three more diverse people standing on my porch in prayer:

17. Ellis, "Five Myths."

Heavenly Father, we know that as humans our knowledge is finite. Please give us wisdom as we read the Bible and other sources you might lead us to. We know how much you love Israel and the Jews. We also know how much you love the Palestinians who've suffered so much. Please raise up a Gandhi-like leader from among their midst. As we come to grips with our differences, help us to love you, to love one another, and to do your will. From everlasting to everlasting, we thank you for your patience, your abundant love, and your infinite understanding. In Jesus' name, we pray, Amen.

Buried Alive

Conversion plays out not in a single cathartic experience but over a lifetime. It had been years since my initial transformation, and life had gotten in the way. Ricocheting between wasted prayer and meaningless therapy, I sensed a malevolent troll working to destroy me in the dark. If I had a heavenly home, I had wandered far from it and couldn't find my way back. Though I continued to pray, write, and meditate, God stayed silent during the years of Michael's drug addiction.

Michael was at UGA, when the phone rang at 2:00 a.m. I said to Steve, "Can you get it? It must be Michael."

I heard him ask, "Are you okay, pal? What do you mean, your grades? Aren't you going to the tutor?"

My pulsed racing, I picked up the phone in the study so that Steve could fall back to sleep. Michael said, "Mom, I'm seeing creatures in the dark, and I'm afraid. Maybe I need to come home for the weekend."

I said, "Of course, I want you to come, honey. Mike, I'm so sorry you're having a hard time. I love you so much."

Softly, he said, "Don't worry, Mom. I guess I'm just overtired." Though I knew that drug use can cause hallucinations, I considered it a waste of breath to ask further questions, ones that would only reinforce an ingrained pattern of lies and defenses. Someone I desperately loved was beyond my reach. I felt the unbearable strain of trying to reason with unreason and creating meaning out of chaos.

We talked for a few more minutes, and I told him that I looked forward to seeing him on the weekend.

I walked back into the bedroom and, seeing Steve still awake, I asked, "How did he seem to you?"

He said, "Oh, I guess okay. His grades aren't good."

"Did he tell you about his hallucinations?"

"No."

"Well, he told me," I said.

"I think he's fine," Steve said. I got little sleep that night and wished that Michael hadn't called. As it turned out, he didn't come home that weekend.

That summer, he lived with two friends in Charleston on Spring Street, at the time the worst neighborhood in the city. We decided not to provide him with any material support. After we took away his car because of unpaid tickets, he broke his ankle in a fall. Every morning, he rose at six and hobbled on his crutches to his job at King Street Station several miles away.

That Michael owed money to several unsavory characters added to these worries. Unable to take in the accumulation of catastrophic concerns, I obsessed over the fact that my dear boy had dyed his beautiful brown hair a horrid shade of orange.

I attended my first Al-Anon meeting during this grueling time. Al-Anon helps family members and friends cope with a loved one's addiction to alcohol or drugs. We met in the Sunday school building adjacent to Shandon Presbyterian Church. I plodded up the steep walkway to the ivy-clad complex, wondering if I would know anyone. I saw only three people in the room. After the perfunctory readings, each person gave a brief history of why they had come. Shirley, an acquaintance from the Jewish community, lived with her alcoholic brother, someone I didn't know. Her pallid complexion and deeply furrowed brows accentuated her gloom. Her pink printed dress, frayed at the edges, reminded me of a Cacharel piece I once owned.

I knew the other man, Dan, from Steve's law school days. Ostensibly, he came because of his girlfriend's alcohol problem, but I knew he drank heavily himself. Jean, who sat beside me, had suffered the ravages of her son's drug addiction for more than twenty years. You couldn't tell by her fine, patrician features—smooth skin, chiseled nose, and high cheekbones. I wondered why only Jewish mothers wore the tracks of emotion on their faces. I had noticed more than a few wrinkles on mine.

Offering an update, Shirley said, "My brother, John, frustrates me to no end. When he's on a drinking binge, he piles his dirty clothes where I can't find them. Then he has the audacity to complain when they are dirty." This trivial complaint caused me to wonder if I'd made a mistake in coming.

Dan said, "Shirley, if he questions you, simply say that you couldn't find them, and don't be mean about it. Treat it as a natural consequence."

Everyone looked at me, but not wanting to give a long history, I talked about Michael's current situation in Charleston.

Jean said, "I've been where you are, and I can't give advice, but I'm just glad you feel free to talk. This group has been a lifesaver for me. We always say that you're only as sick as your secrets."

Dan piped in, "If there's one thing I've learned, it's that attitude is the only thing we can control."

Shirley added, "We have this notion here called loving detachment. You can show compassion without being co-dependent." This came out of my own playbook, so I just nodded.

Jean said, "I've had to compartmentalize the problem and go on with the rest of my life. I don't want to miss out on the good things."

Despite Jean's appearance and demeanor, the stench from her breath repelled me. Magical thinking from an overwrought imagination caused me to wonder if it came from the slow burning of her heart. At the end of the session, she took me aside to give me a copy of a prayer by the Catholic mystic Julian of Norwich.

> God only Desires that our soul cling to Him with all of its strength.
> In particular, that it cling to his goodness. For all of the things our
> mind can think about God, it is thinking upon his goodness that
> pleases Him most and brings the most profit to our soul.[18]

Though Jean's pain penetrated me, her spirituality passed me by like a fading comet. Words about God's goodness might as well have come from a distant planet. I was far from remembering the insights that had once uplifted me. I knew only two things that day: pain had eclipsed my faith, and this would be my last Al-Anon meeting.

When I arrived home, for some unknown reason, I wrapped the Julian of Norwich prayer in heavy layers of linen and placed it for safekeeping deep in a drawer under my lingerie.

Had I stayed with Al-Anon, I would have received the grace I desperately needed. Increasingly, I see the importance of support groups for people with the same caliber of pain. As hard as they tried, Gaye, Lillian, and Laurie couldn't understand my situation. Yet by lifting me up to God, they put me in touch with the only one capable of walking in my shoes. At certain

18. "Goodness." In a Hazelnut: Short Reflections on Julian and Monastic Life (blog), The Order of Julian of Norwich, 2006–2015, https://www.orderofjulian.org/Goodness.

intervals, pride and envy kept me from praying with them. Despite their lofty outpourings on my behalf, hearing their legitimate prayer concerns made me feel worse. I would have gladly traded places with them. When I lacked the energy to pray in return, I felt like a monster. The unbearable gratitude of grace comes to mind when I think of how they saved my life during these difficult years. Though grace can't be repaid, I experience unparalleled joy when I pray for these three families.

Steve and I went through upheavals in which every apparent healing was followed by yet another relapse. I would have preferred one tragic event with its searing aftermath to years of constant anxiety. Dangling between high hopes and low expectations felt far more damning to my soul.

Over time, I came to resent periods of normalcy, ones that set me up and left me with the paradoxical residue of hope. During my darkest times, I winced at hearing others' petitions for me, fearing that hope would gain a foothold and then disappoint. Only now do I see that muscular, solid hope is its own reward—never wasted, regardless of the outcome.

Nothing served to focus my mind for prayer as did Michael's desperate condition. Everyday concerns didn't have enough bite. With no earthly recourse in sight, I simply threw up my hands in total reliance on God. The Bible says, "Hope deferred makes the heart sick" (Prov 13:12). It also cites two ways in which we should pray—one, presuming that God will answer, the other, surrendering to his will. Should I, like the apostle Paul (who prayed only three times), accept this as a thorn in my side? In the delicate dance between presumption and trust, I prayed for the best and prepared for the worst. At the least, I placed my hope on heavenly realities rather than earthly circumstance.

Panic streaked across my dreams, causing me to wake choked with heartache. In one recurring nightmare, I stood in the middle of a battlefield with gunfire coming at me from both directions. Unsure of whom to side with, I laid down and played dead.

During this time, unable to cry, I wrote two poems:

Trauma

silent screams descend

upon my psyche.

worlds dissolve beneath my feet,

as tears of dry debris still the river.

I am a marble statue,

a ghostly figure skulking

in a barren landscape

Dread

Dread lies dormant no more.

Like an ember groping to return,

it searches for root,

my slow, aching core giving fuel evermore.

Coming out of the night, it gains a foothold.

A dense fog invading my mind,

its terror beckons a hundred-fold.

Between threat and promise my numbness resides.

Where cold facts carry their own weight,

my slow, grinding pulse remains.

I try to pray, groping for certitude.

Guide me to a place where tenuous hope erases fear

and creative suffering brings you near.

The steamrolling, cumulative effect of night terrors and anxiety attacks left me in a weakened state. My psychiatrist diagnosed me with post-traumatic stress disorder, PTSD. A situation in real time caused me to overreact, taking me back to a more severe incident in the past. The symptoms of an anxiety attack include chest and stomach pains, headaches, racing pulse, difficulty breathing, profuse perspiration, and numbing throughout the body.

Doctors treated my condition with a form of therapy called EMDR, which stands for eye movement desensitization and reprocessing. Trauma resides on a cellular level in the brain. In recalling troubling memories while engaging in lateral eye movements, they can be transformed. Studies show that people using EMDR can make greater gains than those in years of talk therapy.[19] Later, I benefitted from transcranial magnetic stimulation (TMS), which is used at major medical centers to treat depression and PTSD.

19. "What is EMDR?"

CHAPTER 20

Revealing my Faith: Liberation

AFTER HIS LAST TREATMENT center—Pacific Hills, in Laguna Beach, California—Michael spent two years at Cal State Fullerton, where he completed his BA. He stayed in California for an additional seven years while he worked as a teacher's aide in a special education classroom. Had Michael lived in Columbia when I revealed my faith, embarrassment would have overcome him.

As I gained in maturity and self-awareness, I began to experience the drawbacks of living a solitary inner life. I had integrated my interior and outward realities to the degree that I wanted to live life from my truest, most rooted self. My values had taken on such universal attributes that they overrode many of the cultural norms I had grown up with. I cared less and less about the collective concerns of the Jewish community. Not to have changed course, at this point, would have required greater courage than speaking out in truth.

Because my actions would have consequences for Mom and Dad, I sought their input as much as possible. We had many emotional discussions before they came to understand the difficulties inherent in my situation. I will always cherish their unconditional love and unwavering support in accepting my decision.

I gave warning to my Jewish friends who would undoubtedly face repercussions from my disclosure. I presumed that whatever they felt in the privacy of their own hearts they could discuss among themselves. Because of their support, I count the following as my treasured gems: Susan B., Ina G., Jane K., Barbara B., Peggy J., Penni N., Bev S., Suzie F., and Cindy S. Many Jewish friends subsequently expressed their respect as well.

I cannot recall when or how I let the word out, but when it hit the air, it traveled rapidly. I continued going to Jewish functions where I encountered the slow rumble of disharmony and, at times, outright disdain. Some who when alone greeted me warmly showed downright embarrassment in the presence of others. I chose not to jump into their minds and imagine their thoughts, however understandable. Though the discomfort didn't linger, over the years, I noticed a subtle change in my social demeanor. Instead of approaching others and risking their disapproval, I let them approach me.

Throughout this period, Rabbi Epstein and his wife, Chavi, reached out to me with affection by continuing to invite me to their house. Columbia's Jewish community, my home base, continues to model intellectual achievement, passion for Jewish causes, and concern for the wider cultural community. Today, seventeen years hence, many consider my conversion old news.

During this period, a gentile friend asked, "Gail, how would you label yourself? 'Jewish Christian,' 'Completed Jew,' 'Hebrew Christian,' or 'Messianic Jew?'"

Half seriously, I replied, "God only knows." Without meaning to, I had given her a precise theological answer. Only God can know the variety and subtlety of the problems I have encountered with regard to identity. Only he can name me in a culture that would prefer to box me in.

After trying several Bible study groups, I found a comfortable fit with Lewis Galloway at Shandon Presbyterian Church. I gained from Lewis' creative intellect and his ability to distill complicated ideas down to a single truth. With the ease known only to the truly gifted, he combined biblical knowledge with serious insights from philosophy and literature.

I resonated with Lewis's approach to interpreting Scripture: that of taking it too seriously to take it literally. Many read the Bible as a phone book, attempting to reconcile conflicting passages by fitting them into precise categories. Others, at the opposite extreme, permit so much mystery that they refuse to accommodate any dogma, whatsoever. Reasonable people can disagree on where to draw the line between a solvable problem and a mystery; all things being equal, I contend that it takes greater faith to trust than to know.

Coming to belief from the outside gives me a perspective not available to those who grew up in the church. Always sensitive to Christianity's Jewish roots, I find myself filtering New Testament concepts through the sieve of Jewish perspective. The Book of Acts relates how the early church decided that gentile believers did not have to become Jewish before accepting

Jesus. Years before my baptism, I longed for the church to reverse the favor by not expecting me to convert.

Steve belongs to Holy Trinity Greek Orthodox Church in Columbia, where he has sponsored icons in memory of his parents. Before I opened up about my spiritual transition, Steve went to receive communion at Holy Trinity. The priest shocked him when, in front of hundreds of parishioners, he refused to allow Steve to participate. Humiliated and embarrassed, Steve returned to his seat. Later, he learned that because I hadn't been baptized, the church considered us "unequally yoked."

I said, "You know, Steve, in the first century, Jesus would have welcomed you to the table. Remember, he fought against rigid rules. But why in God's name would you want communion if you don't believe a word of it?"

As usual, he found humor in my studied analysis. Looking self-satisfied, he said, "What do you expect? It's simple. I'm Greek."

When visiting the priest, I revealed my belief and Steve's agnosticism. Dumbfounded by the irony, he laughed so heartily that he fell off his chair. These were his rules, not mine, and I didn't help him up.

Steve often accompanied me to Shandon. Once, I noticed him standing erect, stiffly grabbing the pew in front of him. I said, "Honey, please relax. You look as though you're holding on for dear life." He gave me a knowing smile. Heaven help this dear man if he ever gives up control.

Before my baptism, I couldn't participate in communion at Shandon. Steve, however, took part. One Sunday, he walked back to me with a mischievous grin. Sitting down, he proceeded to open his hand and give me half of his communion wafer.

CHAPTER 21

Mom and Dad

FOR TWENTY-TWO YEARS, WE had the inestimable sorrow of watching Dad decline from Parkinson's disease. Parkinson's is a progressive disorder of the nervous system that affects movement. At first, Dad showed only a minor tremor in his hand. Later, his face showed little or no expression and his arms didn't swing as he walked. As the disease progressed, he had tremors in both limbs and difficulty with posture and balance. His steps became shorter and his feet dragged. A psychiatrist treated him for depression, a common symptom of the disease. After eighteen years, he needed a wheelchair and help with feeding himself. His mind remained keen throughout.

I showed him an article written by someone who feared a similar diagnosis. He wrote that when the neurologist told him he had Parkinson's disease, a small voice assured him that he would find peace. The disease would serve as a conduit to God if he could share with him every tremor and bout of stiffness. I hadn't said a word about Jesus, but the mere association of God with disease clearly rattled Dad. If expressions could ridicule, his most certainly did. It appeared to say, "Why in God's name would you read me such a cockamamie story?" I wouldn't allude to spirituality again until before his death. Incidents like this one increased my understanding of why I had to go outside family to find a relationship with God.

Dad required round-the-clock care. His caretakers gave the household an air of vitality and comradeship, nicknaming Mom "Angel" and Dad "Boss." Mom became an expert on Parkinson's disease, oversaw Dad's eating, vitamins, and medicines, and kept abreast of the latest research. As was her nature, she tracked Dad's progress in copious charts and notebooks.

Dad never complained about his condition. Mom took on so much of his pain that he didn't need to. Knowing that spirituality could lessen her load, I encouraged her to read a favorite book, *The Healer of Shattered Hearts*, by Rabbi David Wolpe. She declined.

To enliven the atmosphere Mom and I collected small stuffed animals and gave them outrageous names. As the inanity steamrolled, we decided to give them a birthday party. As evidence that all joined in, I have pictures of Steve, Dad, and Alan (Dad's primary caretaker), donning birthday hats.

Alan and Dad enjoyed their morning routine of running errands before grabbing lunch. One day, when they returned to the house, Alan took me aside. "Gail, promise you won't tell Angel? I don't want to get Boss in trouble."

With widened eyes, I asked, "Alan, what in the world do you mean?"

Grinning, Alan said, "Boss just cheated on her. We went to Frank's today, and he had two hot dogs."

One day, I met them for lunch at a local seafood shack. I laughed at the sight of their matching jogging suits. Alan, who is African American, said, "We're twins. But there's only one problem. How the heck will anyone tell us apart?"

For Hanukkah one year, Mom wanted a lifelike baby doll called a reborn doll. It had hand-painted features and individually woven strands of authentic hair. Mom gave hers the totally original name of Baby. The reborn-doll fad prompted BBC to produce a documentary about perfectly sane women who talked to them, dressed them, and walked them in fancy carriages.[1]

Over the years, Mom developed obsessive-compulsive disorder, a condition that played havoc with our lives. Her preparation for a weekend trip, for example, began a month in advance, with lists and compilations of toiletries in different colored plastic bags. Her caretakers humored her by complying with unnecessary, time-consuming tasks.

One day, we tried to get her to acknowledge her growing problem. To convince us she wasn't making up superfluous things to do, she invited everyone to examine Baby's fall clothes. Pointing to Baby's skirt and sweater, she said, "I know you'll have to agree with me that these colors don't match. I can't possibly take Baby out like this. Ethel has agreed to take me to the store again to find a sweater that actually matches."

Everyone rolled their eyes. Needless to say, we couldn't discern a difference in hue. After this episode, we stopped trying.

---

1. *My Fake Baby*, http://www.imdb.com/title/tt1179892/.

Mom's Journal:

Gladys once said, "Mrs. Baker, you walk in this house and you feel love." It has sustained us all. Their heart and soul, their tender nursing have created a magical force as if they have waved their restorative wand and ministered. To top it off this is not a house of illness. We laugh, we have fun. We enjoy and celebrate the days in spite of Lee's illness . . . Our wonderful caretakers have kept us going. They are truly our guardian angels, fortifying both Lee and me through incredible stress and sadness.

The baby that Gail ordered arrived today. The undeniable emotion of mother love has been intense as I hold Baby. I am once again Pat, new mother, embracing each of my three girls. It is incredible.

I started an offbeat family tradition centering on the book *Enjoying God*, by A. J. Hill. In it, Hill enumerates passages in the Bible illustrating God's unconditional love.[2] Knowing that Mom would read only the Jewish parts, I set about deleting the Christian passages with scissors, masking tape, and black felt marking pens.

Not wanting to pester her about it, I hadn't known she'd actually read it until years later when I saw the telltale signs: the book had excerpts double and triple underlined in green, red, and purple ink.

One passage spoke of God's unquenchable love for us and how we can't do anything to earn his approval. As perfectionists, both of us had difficulty accepting God's grace. Just as I hated my trademark label, "spacey," she always hated it when people called her "the consummate lady." Maybe she wanted to express a different side of her nature. Over time, she became comfortable using cuss words. In her case, I considered these signals of transcendence. She needed to express the totality of her unladylike self before God.

Another section starred with bullet points told of an unusual adoption story. During the Korean War, a pastor in a small rural Korean village awoke one morning to find that his only child had been killed. The pastor, beside himself with grief, searched for the murderers. Early one morning, he stole into their house and confronted them. "You owe me a debt, and I have come to collect it."

The two men were obviously expecting to be killed in retaliation. But the pastor's next words astonished them. "You have taken my son," he said,

2. Hill, *Enjoying God*.

"and now I want you to become my sons in his place." The two became Christians, went to seminary, and were ordained. Today, they are pastors in Korea—all because of a father who was willing to do whatever it took to win them.[3] From the bullet points embedded in the passage, I assumed Mom felt astonishment at the father's capacity to forgive. I could only hope that she had forgiven God for Dad's Parkinson's disease.

Dad's evolution hit me over the head like a bludgeon. Disease and mortality may have focused his mind, crystallizing insights not available to him earlier. After fifty-five years of perfunctory banter, our communication reached a new level.

When the progression of his disease forced him to quit work, I couldn't hide my tears. He took me aside, saying, "Gail, I know you love me, but seeing you like this only makes me feel worse. You need to remember that the person suffering has resources that you can't see."

From another, these words wouldn't have been so startling, but from him they had the staying power to warm my soul even today. I had to wonder what other aspects of his personality lay buried waiting to be revealed.

Michael made the trip from California to spend quality time with his granddad. I watched as they bonded over sporting events and Michael's extensive baseball-card collection. Once, I overheard a discussion during which Dad said, "God's never done anything good for me." This prompted me to write a poem that I gave to him. After he died, I found it in his personal effects—wrinkled, torn, and frayed at the edges. It reads:

> If I could but take on your pain, would it ease your burden or would it all be in vain? Caring to my soul's outer limit, I can never inhabit your heart—that remains heaven's part.
>
> Only the eternal can break the impasse—your brokenness upon God cast, forever absorbed in identifying love, such as I am incapable of.
>
> A simple sigh and prayerful refrain are all I can give and all that remain:
>
> "God, grant him the gift of faith, his soul to be with thine, a resting place for all of time."

A year later when Janna, Laurie, and I sat beside him giving our last goodbyes, for some reason we erupted into laughter. At first, I felt a level of disquiet about the incident, but, later, I sensed symbolism in the

---

3. Hill, *Enjoying God.*

co-occurrence of laughter and death. Peter Berger, in *Rumor of Angels*, wrote that mirth can signal transcendence when it occurs in the face of acute suffering or death.[4] As with men making music in a city under bombardment, it reflects the ultimate defiance of death.

Mom's Journal:

I was impressed with Lee's acceptance of what he knew was unchangeable—his Parkinson's. The tall erect Lee was no more. To me even in his wheelchair, he is still ten feet tall. Lee's incredible sense of presence and gallantry transcends any physical frailty. His princely bearing and courageous acceptance remind me of grandiose nobility. I am in awe of him.

Lee's death has been difficult—more than difficult. It's hard for me to take pen and write my emotions. I will write an exchange of words Lee and I had a month ago at dusk in our library—I said, "Is there anything you want to tell me?" He said, "I love you very, very much." I said, "And I love you, sweetheart—very, very much." There was silence, when I said, "Is there anything else?" He said, looking out of the library window, "It's getting dark." I said, "You know that I will always be with you, don't you?" He said, "Yes, and that we'll always be together." He nodded his head and with all the beauty, softness, and peace within him, silently smiled. It's probably the nearest Lee ever came to saying good-bye.

4. Berger, *A Rumor of Angels*, 59.

CHAPTER 22

Baptism

AFTER DAD'S DEATH, I made the decision to become baptized. Up to this point, my emotional reservations centered on the fact that for centuries Jews had died rather than endure forced baptism. I also held to the misconception that baptism implied a final severing of ties to the Jewish community. Before, pride may have caused me to identify with Simone Weil, the Jewish Christian mystic who refused to join the church because of anti-Semitism.

I came to see that my Christian commitment connected me not only to a group but to Jesus himself. By revisiting the fact that the early church consisted of both Jewish and gentile believers, I could envision myself on a continuum between the two faiths.

On the day of my baptism, I entered the sanctuary and asked Agnes Norfleet about the Hebrew word for resurrection. She laughed at my capacity for curiosity up to the bitter end. Maybe she thought I needed one more piece of information before going through with the process. We later found out that the English equivalent of the Hebrew word for resurrection is "lifted up." Because the Hebrew language is very concrete, abstract nouns describe actions.

Steve and Michael stood behind me all the way and understood the significance of the process. Agnes made note of my Hebrew name, Avigayil, which means "to give God joy." Heaven willing, I did.

The following words were written into the program:

> Gail, in baptism, God claims you and seals you to show that you belong to Him. God frees you from sin and death, uniting you with Jesus Christ in his death and resurrection. By water and the Holy Spirit, you are made a member of the church, the body of Christ, and are joined to Christ's ministry of love, peace, and justice.

Given your journey of faith through the rich tradition of Judaism to this moment of your Christian Baptism, I have chosen the text from the Torah, from the Book of Deuteronomy: "Hear, O Israel, The Lord is our God, all alone. You shall love the Lord your God with all your heart, and with all your soul and with all your might. Keep these words that I am commanding you today in your heart."

Gail, also hear these words of Jesus Christ: All authority in heaven and on earth has been given to me. Go therefore and make disciples of all nations, baptizing them in the name of Almighty God, and of the Son and of the Holy Spirit, and teaching them to obey everything that I have commanded you. And remember, I am with you always, to the end of the age.

I felt the full force of dying and beginning anew. In sharing in the death and resurrection of Christ, I experienced union, not only through his blood but also through water. God transformed, renewed, and ravished my soul by claiming me through adoption. Remembering Jesus' baptism in the Jordan, I imagined God saying to me, "This is my beloved daughter, Gail, with whom I am well pleased."

After the service, I visited one of my favorite mentors, Ellen Scoville, whose words always elevated me. She had lost two daughters but not her faith. One day, she turned to me and said, "Gail, I don't ever want you to think that God is mean."

When we arrived home, I reminded Steve that his Greek name, *Anastasi*, means resurrection. He couldn't get away from it if he tried. I decided not to share the fact of my baptism with Mom and asked Agnes not to put news of it in the bulletin. Shandon Presbyterian remained my church home for many years.

CHAPTER 23

Mom's Jesus Miracle

THE YEAR AFTER DAD died, Mom faced a series of calamitous health concerns. In addition to near paralysis from a recurrent spinal cyst, she underwent emergency surgery for sepsis in her abdominal cavity. When I greeted her in the recovery room, she was still under the effect of the anesthesia. Looking perturbed, she asked, "I've been waiting for a long time. Gail, where in the world is Lee?"

Stunned into silence, I wondered if I had heard her right. I turned the radio down and asked, "Mom, what did you say about Dad?

Again, she asked, "Why isn't Lee here?"

I stared at her, waiting for some recognition to settle in. In retrospect, I should have asked the nurse to intervene.

I moved closer and held her hands in mine. I swallowed hard and managed to whisper, "Mom, I hate to be the one to tell you, but Daddy passed away almost a year ago."

Glaring at me, she let out a preternatural cry. As the truth sank in, her moans gave way to soft weeping. Then she muttered softly, "Gail, I hope you don't mind. I need to be alone."

After describing the desolate scene to the nurse, she said, "These things are common. I'll keep an eye on her."

She stayed in the hospital for almost two weeks. On the third, and supposedly the worst day after surgery, she was in a morphine stupor. The nurse who had warned me of the medicine's effect said that she might experience hallucinations.

Over the next hour, becoming more alert, she said, "Gail, come closer. Something religious just happened to me." I laughed to myself at her phrasing and moved my chair to her bedside.

She said, "I met, er, a most unusual character—a rabbi who calls himself Jesus. We spent long hours talking about family, and I desperately want to see him again. I think I owe you and Laurie an apology. I was wrong about so many things."

After stifling a guffaw, I began to humor her with polite attentiveness. Because Mom had always bemoaned the fact that both her daughters had left Judaism, I had a hard time trusting her words.

I assumed her Jesus rant would cease when the morphine's effect wore off. However, she continued it throughout her hospital stay and even when she arrived home. Settled in her bed, she looked at me earnestly and said, "Honestly, Gail, Jesus feels so real that I could reach out and touch him. He's brought me closer to my Jewish God."

The stakes rose when she shared her experience with several of her close Jewish friends and invited Rabbi Epstein over. When I greeted him at the door, we looked at each other, stupefied. I exclaimed, "Don't look at me, I had nothing to do with it." (Aside from my prayers, I didn't.)

Sitting next to them in the den, I listened intently as Mom recounted her tale of transformation. With dramatic conviction, she extended one arm, saying, "I'm a Jewess, Rabbi, and I don't know what to do with this new information."

With intriguing and unexpected insight, Rabbi Epstein said, "Only God can control the direction of our spiritual lives." I thought I saw a softening in her facial lines at the prospect of yielding to God's sovereignty. Control had always been Mom's downfall. I'd known that for her to fully access God's grace, she'd have to free herself of this defense mechanism. It's true that Gladys and Ethel had noticed some mellowing in her obsessive ways after she returned home—that is, in every area except her Jesus talk.

Initially, I was reticent about engaging her on the topic. My research on the resurrection indicated that hallucinations rarely produce substantive life change. Over the next few months, however, I began to wonder if God could use any means at his disposal to bring about her spiritual renewal. I had to remember that the greatest miracles might not occur as extravaganzas on mountaintops but in shabby hospital rooms.

Tentatively, I began questioning her about her experience. Over the next six months, we enjoyed uplifting, insightful conversations and savored our newfound camaraderie. Once, in a light-hearted aside, she said, "Gail, sometimes I think Jesus loves me more than he loves anyone in the universe. He's as available to me as anyone who has ever lived or will ever live."

I laughed, saying, "You know, you're right, Mom. I feel that way too. He's as close to me as my right hand." She had accessed such an infinite connection that she understood that heaven's mathematics is not a zero-sum equation.

I said, "Why don't we design T-shirts with the words, 'Jesus loves me best?'"

Every morning, I came to her house where we read the Psalms together and then prayed. On a clear day in early December, a remark from Mom forced me to confront something that will forever mystify and confound me. I still remember the churning sensation in my stomach.

Waiting for her in the kitchen, I looked outside, marveling at the multitude of sparrows cutting a wide swath across the blue-gray horizon. She came in dressed in a blue-and-white sweater with jeans. After discussing her plans for the day, I said, "Mom, I've picked out a psalm for us to read. What would you like to pray about, today?" Looking at me with tepid, uncertain eyes, she said, "Gail, I don't want to talk about God, today. Maybe, tomorrow."

Tomorrow never came. The more I persisted, the more she balked. Every time I mentioned Jesus, she scoffed as though spurning a lost lover. I wondered if someone in the Jewish community had spoken to her. For reasons known only to God, her grand alteration ended as suddenly as it had begun. After having ingested every morsel of numinous love Jesus could possibly avail to her, she dropped him cold. Finally, realizing that I couldn't compete with the dark force gripping her, I stopped trying altogether.

Over the next six years, Mom's health showed considerable improvement. During this time, I continued to pray that God would renew her spirit. She couldn't have been at greater risk. None of us knew what she would have to endure over the next stage of her life.

CHAPTER 24

Interim Years

Humor

MICHAEL, NEARING THIRTY, DECIDED to return to Columbia. He loved working as a property manager and interacting with Steve in the real-estate business. In addition to reconnecting with aunts and cousins, he studied with Rabbi Epstein. He dated often and socialized with a group of young Jewish professionals. A talented painter, he joined a local arts group.

Over this period, Steve and I made the most of every reprieve that came our way. As I put it, we grabbed bliss by enjoying each other and new friends in the community. My friends continued to be so varied and interesting that I discouraged them from planning a sixtieth birthday party: With Buddhist, Christian, and atheist buddies all spanning the liberal-conservative political divide, I feared World War III might erupt if they chanced to engage in serious conversation.

Several of those close to me have admitted to not having a spiritual bone in their body. It matters not. But, sensitive to this, I compartmentalize and interact from my secular zone. (Living with Steve has afforded me considerable practice.) Though I refrain from religious jargon, I voice my convictions when asked. Once, a gentile friend said, "Gail, I just don't like religious people." I responded, "You'd get along great with Jesus. He didn't either."

One of my favorite ways to bond is to spend the afternoon with longtime family friends, Carla and Cyd. With the wisdom of age and a lightness of spirit, they stimulate a deep reservoir of happy impressions to which we return again and again. The give and take of our conversations resembles a sacred bond. Recounting generational sagas of things that fell apart and came together again, we crisscross time, clinging to our common sense of belonging.

The comedian Chris Rock suggested that comedy is the blues for people who can't sing.[1] Despite Michael's progress, the years of stress had taken their toll on me. Because I couldn't sing, I craved comic relief.

I had tongues wagging for weeks about a practical joke I orchestrated at my niece Rebecca's birthday party. In the lounge of an upscale country club, Rebecca and I, along with her friends, feigned passing out from too much to drink. Stretched on chaises surrounded by empty liquor bottles, we stifled laughter as dismayed guests sauntered past us to use the facilities.

When Sarah Spotts, head of the Hebrew school, strode in demanding, "Is there an adult in charge?" We knew that the charade had ended. Though my young cohorts would talk about the episode for years, some of their parents scratched their heads in disbelief over my judgment.

I became enthralled with a practical-joke website called Improv Everywhere, a New York City comedy collective that stages unexpected performances in public places. Created by Charlie Todd, of Columbia, they surprise random strangers through positive pranks, or "missions." Since 2001, they have staged more than 150 projects involving tens of thousands of undercover performers.

Community Involvement

Though Michael was appreciably better in many areas, his frequent bouts of depression kept me in a state of anxiety. During these intervals, I volunteered at Life Care nursing home. By focusing on others, I hoped to find meaning and forget my worries.

On the first day, I entered a cheerful facility with beautiful fabrics and antique-looking furniture. The volunteer coordinator guided me toward the arts-and-crafts room where I would engage dementia patients with creative therapies. My first client, a ninety-five-year-old woman, had just fallen out of her wheelchair onto the floor. As I helped her up, she looked at me with fierce determination and said, "If my Daddy were here, this never would have happened."

Art had a transformative impact on these patients. The documentary *I Remember Better When I Paint* shows how painting and drawing can improve quality of life by awakening a patient's self-esteem.[2] It shouldn't have surprised me that the process enabled me to move forward as well.

1. "Quotes by Chris Rock," https://www.coolnsmart.com/author/chris_rock/.
2. Ellena and Huebner, *I Remember Better.*

Volunteering also with Palmetto AIDS Life Support Services (PALSS) and Palmetto Health Hospice, I saw firsthand how impending death could focus a client's mind. I believe I raised the level of communication in saying, "I don't have anything over you. Sooner or later, I'll be in your shoes. It's only a matter of time."

Steve chaired the boards of the Baker and Baker Concert Series at the Columbia Museum of Art as well as the Salvation Army. I chaired the South Carolina State Museum's foundation and served on the boards of the Library Foundation and LRADAC, a group that deals with drug addiction and prevention.

In 2014, Canon Patsy Malanuk and I organized a seminar on religious persecution at Trinity Episcopal Cathedral. This event bridged my divergent interests. Before an audience of Christian and Jewish friends, Patsy and I interviewed sons of Holocaust survivors. Afterward, several of us spoke about the anti-Semitism we encountered growing up in Columbia. Church groups began reading Rabbi Jonathan Sacks' *The Dignity of Difference*[3] and Amy-Jill Levine's *The Misunderstood Jew*.[4]

It took only a short time for me to decide to join Trinity. Though the irony puzzled Steve, it couldn't have taken God by surprise. This fancy downtown church, which I once associated with snobbery and bigotry, has come to fulfill my every need. My weekly meetings with a group of like-minded women have given me the intellectual nourishment and camaraderie I desperately needed.

Tending the Home Fires

The normal load of life's stress can confound even the best of relationships. The added strain of worrying about Michael led to moodiness, frayed nerves, and disagreements over how to parent. I preferred using natural consequences rather than punishment, and Steve worried about my pattern of disengagement. Early on, Michael, seeing our disparity, used it to his advantage by manipulating us.

Thanks to counseling and considerable mellowing on both of our parts, Steve and I have managed to banish the disquiet and carve out a space of renewal, affection, and humor.

One night before bed, Steve asked, "Have you had a good life?"

3. Sacks, *Dignity of Difference*.
4. Levine, *Misunderstood Jew*.

Not knowing exactly what this might mean to a here-and-now, eat-drink-and-be-merry person, I answered, "I've had a meaningful life—maybe not easy, but one that gives me great satisfaction. Besides, I have you, and that makes it all worthwhile."

"So you're glad you married me?" he asked.

Burrowing my head in the crevice of his neck, I said, "Yes, and you're good for my immune system."

Containing his laughter, he said, "You're the funniest person I've ever met in my life. Is this something else you've researched?"

"Well, yes. The new Harvard study on longevity and happiness confirms that meaningful relationships strengthen blood cells. It just confirms what I've always said: 'All's well that ends well.' Oh, and, Steve, I just have to tell you one more thing. You're my number one man in this world."

He said, "Well, with that, I think we'll call it a night."

Therapy with Michael

Michael, nearing forty, expressed the desire to work on our relationship. With great trepidation, I fully engaged with him in therapy. I will always remember his first comment: "Even horrible men in prison feel they have at least one person who loves them—their mother. I don't even have that. If you wonder why I date older women, it's because you never gave me any affection."

I began to tremble. With faltering words, I said, "Michael, I don't have any way to undo it. At one point, I just zoned out, and don't forget, I got such bad advice.

"I take full responsibility, Michael. For whatever reason, I couldn't break the spell Dr. M. had on me. When I wondered if my prayers about whether to stay or not had been wasted, a wise soul said, 'A decision made in prayer will be either blessed or redeemed.' My decision to stay with Dr. M. was clearly not blessed. Michael, no one loves you more than I do. I see my flaws. Can you ever find it in your heart to forgive me?"

Michael said, "Someday soon, Mama, it will be redeemed. I just know it. We just have to wait."

He was right. We had to wait. Though our relationship took time to heal, therapy, while emotionally exhausting, proved beneficial to both of us.

During this time, Michael showed me the following entry he posted on Facebook:

I had a hard night tonight. Nineteen years ago (plus two weeks,) I entered a rehabilitation facility in the mountains of North Carolina for treatment. I was gravely ill, anorexic, and addicted to the worst form of cocaine. The counselors told my parents to let go of me and plan for my funeral. They did not.

My mother, a spiritual woman, sees meaning in suffering and believes no pain is ever wasted. She always said that I would grow into a strong man who would share her vision of G-d with those suffering as I once suffered. She imagined that I would care for the lost ones on the other side of Spring Street in Charleston.

It was an impossible vision. Spring Street has long since been gentrified, and I view the world through the Jewish lens she gave birth to, not the Messianic lens she has adopted. Though an impossible vision, it wasn't a false vision. Tonight, I gave life to it.

I have a friend, a single mother. She and her child's father suffer with the same addiction I once had. They know the impossibility of this plague, one spread intentionally like a blanket infested with small pox. It is meant to cripple a generation of all who stand in the way of manifest destiny.

Tonight, as I spent time with the father, I could give no measure of comfort or love that would end the night any other way than it was destined to end. After saying goodbye, he walked into the abyss again. I will continue to sit by as I watch friends walk hopelessly into the sea. Like characters in a Kate Chopin novel, they awaken small pieces of my stone heart.

Recognizing my need for escape from the grind of counseling, Steve planned a trip to Rome and Florence. Seeing different scenery energized my spirits and piqued my imagination. Life's purpose seemed simpler when I saw that people everywhere, at work or at play, have the same needs and concerns.

A famed cathedral in its gilded splendor couldn't summon the sort of mystical rapture I experienced at a lowly dungeon site associated with St. Paul. Somehow, I couldn't imagine Jesus being comfortable in the ambiance of the former. On earlier trips, I faced the uncomfortable decision about where to go first—the Jewish section or a renowned cathedral. This time, I felt more settled, with the distinctions not causing disquiet. In Rome, we visited an ancient synagogue in the former Jewish ghetto area where Pope John Paul II gave his famous conciliatory message to both faith communities.

Tony Hiss, in his book *Deep Travel*, wrote that when we savor a vivid memory, we prolong time.[5] Once, flying west to visit Michael, I luxuriated in a sustained view of a maroon, magenta, and gold sunset. I will always remember the exalted expression of a destitute man in San Francisco as he fed peanuts to a flock of hungry pigeons that enveloped him. It's possible that all for the love of one of God's creatures, he could have spent his last dime to nourish them.

By living in the moment with gratitude and wonder, Hiss wrote, we can cultivate what he called "open-sesame" moments, even when we arrive home. I began looking at familiar landscapes in Columbia as if seeing the city for the first time.

Steve and I were in Paris on All Saints' Day, when Christians around the world commemorate their dead. Leaving a museum, we encountered a magical musical procession that started at Notre-Dame and wound its way through the streets. We were standing in respectful silence when, all at once, Steve dodged through the processional to the other side of the avenue.

Our differences fascinated me. Engrossed in the mystical elements and pageantry, I had no concept of time. Steve, knowing we had a rendezvous with friends, moved in their direction. His linear style of thinking causes him to see the destination as the journey. Conversely, my lateral style means I see the journey as an end in itself.

5. Law, "Exchange."

CHAPTER 25

Mom: Alzheimer's and Spiritual Renewal

ON A DAY WITH the sky blue and the smell of hyacinths in the air, everything began to crumble. I picked up the phone to hear the news that Mom was experiencing her first signs of memory loss.

We remained cautiously optimistic, refusing to jump to any conclusions. Fearing a possible Alzheimer's diagnosis, we refrained from mentioning the A word altogether. Many patients lose so much function from the outset that they never reach the stage of conscious acceptance. Mom, as it happened, had complete awareness of every waning facility.

I watched her cross the pulverizing line between hope and despair. Knowing that her mind would eventually fade, she saw no point in trying to retrieve words or fogging remembrances. As her ability to communicate ground to a standstill, she withdrew, taking with her all reassurance and hope. At this point, her doctor treated her for depression.

Having few words of consolation, I could only hope that my presence would bring her a small measure of comfort. I couldn't fathom a purpose behind a disease that annihilated the very fabric of brain needed for prayer. My spiritual questioning took on a life of its own, making the circumstance more difficult to bear. I craved the certainty that God controlled every strand in the gray web choking her brain. The fear of his absence, like holy terror, became the substance of my dark night.

In long impassioned pleas, I placed her next to Jesus. Here, her unadorned presence before God superseded every cherished ability cultivated over a lifetime. I pictured her tears, bountiful and extravagant, as they cascaded over her hands and erased all signs of age. This vision became fixed in my mind and embedded in my dreams.

One morning, I sat with Mom near the hummingbird garden planted on her side lawn. She wore a pale-blue shirtwaist dress and a wide-brim straw hat. Her wispy curls framed a perfect heart-shaped face. With delicate features set on a flawless complexion, she had the kind of beauty that required little deliberate attention.

Mesmerized at the scene before us, we watched as an iridescent ruby-throated hummingbird sipped nectar from a row of midnight-blue salvias. Only a quarter-inch long, its pointed bill moved backwards from flower to flower. In the sun, its beaded wings glistened like sapphires.

Watching the bird hover as if in a time warp, I reminded her that hummingbirds, with their wingspan in the shape of an infinity symbol, represent eternity in Jewish mystical thought. For years, Mom had focused on the marvel and wonder of birds, sharing her enthusiasm with anyone who would listen. Suddenly, with tears streaming down her face, she cried out, "Oh, Gail, you just said it, but I can't even remember. Tell me its name again, please."

I said, "It's a hummingbird, my precious." The back of my neck tightened as her pain gripped me. "Mom, you need to listen carefully to what I'm about to say." Her eyes, deep pools of crystalline love, stared inquisitively at mine.

Words I'd never before formulated, or even conceived of, began flowing from my lips. Slowly, I said, "Mom, whatever you lose in memory or confusion, God will replace with spirit."

Realizing the profundity of what I had so glibly expressed, I repeated the words so as not to forget them. Over the next year, we recanted them as a prayerful refrain until they became self-fulfilling. I will never fathom the parameters of her affliction or the alchemy by which God fashioned meaning out of it. I only know that as she beat down the corridors of heaven she carried me along, a willing participant. Mom, the wounded healer, became the sole person to heal my spiritual insufficiency.

When Mom became comfortable with God's presence in her life, she warmed to prayer as a way of working through her anxiety. We enjoyed relaxed, brutally honest conversations during which I never mentioned the name of Jesus.

The concept of God's providence gave her the assurance that he controlled every fading cell in her brain. When she forgot something, she said, "Well, God must not want me to remember." I heard her greet people with, "You know, I have Alzheimer's, but I still have my spirit, and I still have my soul." Many were so uplifted that I said to her, "Mom, you're God's gift to Alzheimer's disease."

She had always rhapsodized about the artistry and elegance of nature, exhibiting a mystic sense of surprise at every flower, cloud, or sunset. Now, she believed for a fact that the sun rose and set for her alone. Even in her diminished capacity, she expressed gratitude for every good thing in God's creation. Noting her insatiable capacity for wonder, I determined that I would see every familiar blessing as if for the first time.

Her short-term memory loss had some humorous benefits. She often called to leave short, loving messages on our recorder. Forgetting that she had done so, she'd record a second, third, and fourth message, all within two-minute intervals. I'd allot considerable phone time when I recounted happy news about Michael. As if in a surreal game, I'd recap it just to hear here her excited response.

Seldom do I witness another's yielding as a result of my prayers. Through a neural pathway separate from her frontal cortex, Mom developed a conscious connection to God. Her radical surrender reflected not so much blind resignation, but full-bodied resolve. It astonished me that she could relinquish control so easily after having relied on it. Of course, it could be said that Mom took charge of the precise way she wanted to leave this world.

Jews have long accessed this timbre of religious devotion. How it differs in kind or degree from that of devout Christians I will never attempt to guess. Did she have a silent but ongoing relationship with Jesus? Even if she had consciously denied him years ago, her prior knowledge would dwell in the mind of God forever. Regardless, I had to take her at her word. She said that Jesus brought her closer to her Jewish God.

I often think about Mom's last prayer as her mind shut down. Without the impediments of time, worry, control, or choice, she would have simply yielded over the last full measure of her heart's desire. I find it useful in my own meditation to assume this posture.

One night, during the time of Mom's spiritual renewal, I read from John (12:24): "Truly, truly, I say to you, unless a grain of wheat falls into the earth and dies, it remains alone; but if it dies, it bears much fruit." I had the following dream:

> Friday, a fierce thunderstorm struck Mom's neighborhood. Arriving to survey the damage, I found nature holding its breath in

curious stillness. The front yard looked refreshed and lush with a many-textured profusion of greenery. Walking into the back, I saw it had taken the full brunt of the storm.

I found Mom meditating in her usual spot, a half-demolished oak stump she called her "giving tree"—the name taken from Shel Silverstein's book of the same name. Considering the ground adjacent to her giving tree as sacred turf, she'd brought in truckloads of fertile alluvial soil to undergird it. As a nature mystic, Mom believed that every created thing had a primal soul reflecting the divine fingerprint.

When she rose to check the condition of a damaged elm, I saw a face contorted with dark lines of grief. Suddenly, in a bizarre fit of rage she grabbed fistfuls of soil and began vigorously rubbing them over her extremities. Between sobs, she said, "I need their power, Gail. This damn storm messed with my marrow, my inner core. These trees were immortal. Now they're just like me."

After she calmed down, we sat together on a low bench. Heaving a deep sigh of relief, she extended her arms to the sky and said, "Oh, well, what I can't control I'll just hand over to God."

As the bluish haze of dusk settled all around, I watched the fading sun cast a glow on the wasted terrain.

At the close of the dream, Mom started weeping again. Rubbing my eyes to ensure they weren't deceiving me, I saw my prayer vision being played out: Profuse tears fell onto her hands, changing them into the innocent hands of a child.

After drying her eyes, she turned to me and asked, "Gail, can we light the Shabbos candles tonight? I want to thank God for all that remains." As we gathered our belongings and walked toward the house, I considered that the ground around us was consecrated.

The following excerpt from Mom's journal illustrates her passionate connection to the natural world, trees in particular.

Sometimes I awake at night and walk into the den and visit with my tall, towering, majestic pine, silhouetted against a silent sky, outside our window. I seem to gain sustenance and comfort from that wonderful, strong, compassionate tree. It listens with friendship and understanding. I am able to vent my thoughts, cry, communicate, rage, or say whatever comes to mind. It is a spiritual experience that somehow cleanses and keeps me in touch with the healing me. I feel its listening life—its willingness to accept anything I feel . . . I feel like I'm in the middle of a logging camp— large logs piled askew, each other in chaotic array, high brush piles of green pine crowns, bare, raw tree stumps, oozing pine resin. The smell and sound of destruction predominate . . . chain saw, stump grinding, trucks lifting and loading logs—all modern technology to get the job done. In a day or two all evidence will be removed. For some, it won't be known that 20 tall pines once lived here. I shall always know.

I just came from a tranquil visit to my giving tree out back. The scene was a little different. Fallen branches from the pines and their stump were all around. The water below looked clean and pristine. In the sweeping moment. I heard a bird whose voice was new . . . were there an outdoor orchestra, his place would be the napping of castanets. I counted the rings of two fallen logs—not too scientific or exact, they appeared to be 45 and 100 years old—I saw on 2/3 of our tall majestic pine standing so erect. I was reminded of the Indian totem pole and the reverence felt by Native Americans.

CHAPTER 26

Ground Zero

DAD HAD BEEN GONE for six years and Mom's condition had begun to stabilize. After Michael's drug years, he visited Mom often. I watched them snuggle on the couch for long intervals. Mom loved lavishing her affection as much as Michael relished receiving it.

Suspended between the highs and lows of faith, I remained in a static state with a quotidian awareness of God's presence. Despite therapeutic breakthroughs with Michael, I was still anxious about another downturn. I prayed that if the world turned dark again, God would sustain me with a new conversion or a baptism of the spirit. The disparity between these lofty expectations and reality would never be so great as during the coming months. I saw that my capacity for doubt was commensurate with my capacity for faith.

My personal ground zero happened on a day like any other, except for an incessant downpour. I watched as rain pummeled insipient spring, forcing the azaleas' purple and pink wisps to the ground. I realized I would have to wait for the rains to subside before planting my recently purchased dahlia bulbs.

I never saw spring that year. The bulbs remained in the garage until fall, when I discovered them rotting in a dark corner.

I had started to prepare supper when Michael surprised me with a visit. Standing on tiptoes to kiss him, I noticed he wore a yellow raincoat similar to the one he owned as a child. As he cleaned the mud off his shoes, I warned him about flash floods and asked, "Michael, do you remember the floods in our old neighborhood? You and your friends loved playing near the creek. I think you were in third grade."

He said, "I don't remember anything good that year. That's when things started going downhill."

I said, "You must have had some good times."

"I came over because I need to get something out. It's time I told you about something bad that I did."

"What do you mean, Michael?"

He looked away for a moment. When our eyes met again, I saw an expression of shame and embarrassment. The blood drained from my face as I asked, "What happened, honey? You can tell me."

"Mom, there was a stranger in the woods near our house."

My knees buckled as I reached for the chair. I said, "Come sit down with me, Michael. Who was he? I hope he didn't hurt you."

As if talking about the weather or the time of day, he said, "The man made me take off my clothes."

"Oh, my God, Michael. What did he do to you?"

His face looked ashen. He said, "I don't want to say anything else."

I said, "Michael, you know you can trust me. If something bad happened, you were just a kid. It wasn't your fault. You didn't do anything wrong. That man did."

I had to remember to breathe. Every nerve in my body went numb, and I lost all sense of time. The part of me that died that afternoon never revived. Dazed and disoriented, I couldn't compute anything said after this point.

Later, as Steve and I talked about Michael's trauma, we could finally connect the dots with understanding. His symptoms—the sudden lack of motivation, obsessive eating, and recalcitrant behavior—all occurred at the time of his sexual abuse. What began as an ordinary day in our boy's childhood became one in which the imponderable pulled us into a vortex of enigmatic gloom. The telescoped potential of a thousand dreams splintered as the unthinkable finally became thinkable.

Michael's words:

> It was a total system failure. You'd think a teacher or a guidance counselor or one of my many therapists would have asked if anyone had touched me inappropriately. It's kind of a checklist item. I guess they thought I was too fat to get molested. I might as well been wearing a sign. Only the pretty boys and girls get properly molested. I blame society.

Looking back, I can see that perhaps Steve and I failed to provide an atmosphere conducive to honest communication. Had he been able to share his abuse from the outset, we could have seen that he obtained the help he needed. I tremble at the thought of other mistakes we made that caused him difficulty.

Despite gaining closure, we agonized over what our dear boy had endured. He felt unworthy of love and of every good thing that might come his way. To protect himself from shame and powerlessness, he fractured his personality and built up layers of control. I witnessed vulnerability and resilience as he pushed against an impenetrable wall of anger and grief. Though I kept telling him, "No pain is wasted," in my hungering dark I had difficulty believing it. I longed to tell him that Jesus, too, was victimized and that only a God with wounds can truly understand our own.

The pain isolated me from friends. Though I longed for comfort, Michael deserved privacy, and I feared saying too much. My jealousy extended to the entire universe of parents whose sons hadn't been robbed of innocence and personhood.

My anger at the victimizer became a seething, incendiary wound. Pure insurgent rage charged through every vein in my body. I had overcome much, but this stood in a category by itself. Everyone has a breaking point, and I had reached mine. Searching for my imagined sanctuary, I found no one at home. I felt as though my soul had plummeted fathoms into a pit beyond God's reach.

Every drop of spiritual awareness evaporated into thin air. God appeared to be little more than an imaginary childhood friend, an illusory force to cry to. I would have preferred not having loved him at all than to lose him this way. That a single, sinister act could so damage our family caused me to feel at the mercy of malevolent, random forces. Aside from God's sovereignty and the power of Jesus' resurrection, I had nothing to counterbalance it.

I assumed that all of my prayers had amounted to little more than whistling in the dark. I feared losing faith in the same way that I obtained it, this time not as a flash of transcendent insight but as the intuitive cry of my naked soul.

CHAPTER 27

Overcoming Spiritual Despair:
Hope in the Dark

THOUGH, TODAY, I CAN see God's hand at work, at the time, I plowed through what John of the Cross called the "dark night of the soul." Bereft of every grounding delight found in communion with God, I felt adrift and alone in an alien universe.

Time was suspended and meaningless. I sensed that for as long as the stars graced the heavens and the moon stemmed the tides I would dread the appalling sovereignty of God. I placed Julian of Norwich's prayer under my pillow—I could only hope that its meaning would seep deep into my consciousness.

Reading Psalm 88, I gained comfort from the fact that another had waded through waters as deep as mine:

O Lord, my God, I call for help by day;

I cry out in the night before thee.

Let my prayer come before thee,

incline thy ear to my cry!

For my soul is full of troubles,

and my life draws near to Sheol.

I am reckoned among those who go down to the Pit;

I am a man who has no strength,

like one forsaken among the dead,

like the slain that lie in the grave,

like those whom thou dost remember no more,

for they are cut off from thy hand.

Thou hast put me in the depths of the Pit,

in the regions dark and deep.
Thy wrath lies heavy upon me,
and thou dost overwhelm me with all thy waves.
Thou hast caused my companions to shun me;
thou hast made me a thing of horror to them.
I am shut in so that I cannot escape;
my eye grows dim through sorrow.
Every day I call upon thee, O Lord;
I spread out my hands to thee.
Dost thou work wonders for the dead?
Do the shades rise up to praise thee?
Is thy steadfast love declared in the grave,
or thy faithfulness in Abaddon?
Are thy wonders known in the darkness,
or thy saving help in the land of forgetfulness?
But I, O Lord, cry to thee;
in the morning my prayer comes before thee.
O Lord, why dost thou cast me off?
Why dost thou hide thy face from me?
Afflicted and close to death from my youth up,
I suffer thy terrors; I am helpless.
Thy wrath has swept over me;
thy dread assaults destroy me.
They surround me like a flood all day long;
they close in upon me together.
Thou hast caused lover and friend to shun me;
my companions are in darkness.

In the treacherous space where love can twist into hate, I pushed the void into itself and found light. I'd assumed God was so involved in my circumstance that he warranted culpability. I couldn't have it both ways. If I wanted to access his healing touch in my pain, I had to accept his will in every circumstance—good or bad.

Acknowledging his sovereignty became my safe harbor. Unable to grasp how sovereignty, free will, and prayer coalesced, I tilted towards the theology that says, "God allows what he hates to accomplish what he loves." The more I focused my anger at Satan, the more I could access God's goodness.

Clinging to Jesus, I left behind all hope of reward save intimacy with him. Like a moth approaching a flame, I drew close to the object of my desire, finding release in self-surrender. I cultivated a prayer life consisting of more than the mere voicing petitions. I, once, attained such a state of ecstatic union that I envisioned an invisible barrier opening up in the heavens—breaking in as a sonic boom would interrupt time. Without striving for hope or proper sacred feelings, I simply abided with Jesus in his forsaken posture. As with a metaphorical boomerang, faith returned of its own accord.

I expressed this in a journal entry:

> Though in the wilderness of emotional collapse, my spirit remains strong. Jesus inhabits my soul and every other for whom hope has become a paradoxical and mixed metaphor.
>
> His last words of forsakenness serve as a spiritual balm, a veritable homeland for my soul. It is here that I hang my earthly hat when pitiable sorrow descends. Knowing that He voiced them at a time when God was never so near, enables me to trust in the reality of heaven over and above mere circumstance.

In the story of *The Velveteen Rabbit,* a boy's love caused his toy rabbit to morph into a living one.[1] In my earlier despair, I thought of Jesus as nothing more than an imaginary childhood friend to cry to. With faith restored, I mused that by reversing the process, I loved him back into tangible, authentic existence.

1. Williams, *Velveteen Rabbit.*

CHAPTER 28

Losing Mom

NATURALLY, I DIDN'T TELL Mom about Michael's revelation. Her condition had deteriorated to the point that she wouldn't have understood it anyway. Unable to visit her during the worst of my downturn, I'd feigned a sprained ankle. Having regrouped considerably, Steve and I decided to take another trip. We arranged for Mom's care and spent a week in Spain. When we returned home, Mom's worsening condition shocked us: she couldn't remember where we had been and why we left her. Sitting at her kitchen table, I said, "Mom, Steve brought you some pictures of some of Joan Miró's masterpieces."

She glanced at them with little enthusiasm and changed the subject. "Gail, I've been meaning to tell you something about that man you believe in. I forget his name."

"Do you mean Jesus?" I asked.

"Yes. That's him, and I'm happy you have him. Maybe he's not far away from me either. I did love him at one time, you know."

Stunned at her remembrance, I said, "Yes, Mom, I remember well." I reached for her hand and said, "Mom, whatever you believe, God loves you and understands."

Peering down at her diamond ring she asked, "Where is Lee?" Everyone looked puzzled, unsure how to respond.

I said, "Oh, my precious, it's okay. You must have forgotten. Dad died over six years ago."

This was our last semi-cogent conversation. Everyone in the family considered it a blessing when she died of pneumonia a month later. Going through her journals several weeks after the funeral, I discovered a small purple envelope with the label, "My Last Words." Her remarks were true to form, especially in the way they were imparted—undoubtedly written long before she faded:

> In reviewing my last few journal entries about Lee and the girls and life—I find us to be a remarkably human, resilient family who has embraced life with tenderness and passion. Our heartaches and happiness, triumphs and tragedies have awakened within us the courage to be ourselves. We have discovered and are still discovering the truth, the reverence and mysteries of life, I find myself quite often seeking advice and insight from our Gail, our Janna, and our Laurie. I know it will be filled with wisdom and kindness.
>
> Within this whole equation of life is the comfort and calm of God's love. We cannot drift beyond His Love and care. I'd love to stay around to see the next generation. God knows and is smiling. In celebration of the great dance of life, I feel at peace.

Over the next year, I learned how the torment of grief causes a craziness all of its own. My heart felt shattered into a million fragments. The very one I needed to comfort me was nowhere around. Once, joking with Mom, I said, "Someday we may see each other in the resurrection, but you may not recognize me. I may have manicured red nails and blond hair." It was funny then but not now. When a loved one dies, the veil between this life and the next becomes too thin for comfort.

Only after Mom died, when I felt unencumbered by the everyday quirks of her personality, could I fully grasp the essence of her character. I took on the full measure of Mom's emotions over her lifetime. Although she had earned the peace of having loved well and loved in return, she had also endured great sorrow.

At the year mark, I let out every ounce of rage locked in my system—in soulful, visceral cries, I confessed to God that my tears, even if shed in perpetuity, would never touch the core of my loss.

Like defining blue to a man born blind, words fail to describe God's presence. It began as an inner warmth and grew into a palpable certainty. God blessed me by giving his permission for me to cry forever and a day, if need be. In one stellar instant, I knew that only he, the keeper of all memories, could know the precise nature of who and what I had lost and, most important, only he could heal me. I hadn't asked for consolation, but received it nonetheless. It has been ten years since I surrendered my grief and, remarkably, I haven't cried a day since.

Soon afterward, our family engaged a filmmaker to create a short film about Mom's love of nature. Because of difficulties with a large screen we couldn't feature scenes of the woods behind her house. Watching the film-maker's attempts, I half-seriously called out, "Come on, Patricia, I know you're hanging around. Give us some help."

After the filming, Michael and I were loading up the camera equipment when a violent thunderstorm erupted. We watched as craggy bolts of light-ning streaked across the sky and furious maroon clouds released a torrent of hail. Then, remarkably, we saw effervescent shafts of sunlight begin to peak on the lake's horizon. I voiced, "God, please give us a rainbow."

Soon afterward, a rainbow formed over Mom's favorite outdoor piece sculpted by Janna's former husband, Don Creech. Having invoked her pres-ence all weekend, I felt Mom's spirit touching my soul. I had the irrevocable assurance that death, the impenetrable barrier, no longer separated us.

The next week, on Easter Sunday, from my will and not my heart, I prayed: "God, please reach down and touch Michael's victimizer. Draw him to yourself and give him a spirit of repentance. Don't let him hurt another family the way he has hurt ours."

In praying this, I realized that forgiveness entails a kind of dying to self, a releasing of the ego's unhealthy need to settle the score.

CHAPTER 29

The Blessings of an Imperfect Life

IN THE COMINGS AND goings of God's spirit, I've learned that every time I think I'm doing something for God, my visage appears staring me right in the face. I trust that, one day, the mirror will capture his glow, rather than the dim shadow of my own ego. I have also learned that God bestows faith as a gift. Without the ability to muster it on my own, waiting keeps me from pride.

My chronicle describes the ebb and flow of what many call doubt, though I'd prefer to call it "distance." Stemming more from differing moods than any lack of mental conviction, my feelings about God can be distinguished from my thoughts about him. Faith is not a once-and-for-all mental ascent. Like a muscle, it requires strengthening and nourishing on a daily basis

Simone Weil wrote, "Only two things can pierce the human heart— one is affliction and the other is great beauty."[1] Increasingly, it's not the ugly that unsettles me but the beautiful. The full complement of my sad tears has seen its day. Only when a splendid insight grips my core does the stream begin to unlock.

As I look back, time divides into two realities—before and after Michael's horrific unraveling. When spiritual despondency overtook my mind, God transfigured the language of loss into the language of grace. Along the way, I learned that God wastes no amount of world-weariness, desolation of spirit, or grievous remorse in his economy.

This narrative, a plot unfolding, reflects varying selves, some vanishing and some evolving. The recollections, like snapshots of time congealed in a collage, have no importance in themselves. Only when refracted as hindsight do they attain significance because of one essential fact: from the very

1. Moore, "Walking Far."

beginning, I confronted an unknown future. Today, nearing seventy and contemplating the last curtain's descent, I savor the awe and wonder of the process, fully embracing the journey as the destination.

I glance at a picture of me as a toddler, replete with ruffles, doe eyes, and an innocent smile. How could I have known at the time the terrible circumstances I would endure? Likewise, I couldn't know the luminous path I would take, one leading not to a nostalgic home of diminished stature but to a heavenly one where God redeems all suffering and makes the world whole again.

I turn to a recent shot of Michael, noticing that his erect muscular build conveys authority and confidence. Along with darkly handsome features, I discern on his countenance knowledge that he is radically beloved by God. The handiwork of his stung heart, ever brave, cradles my soul.

Some mornings, I am bone weary and befuddled by the complications of my messy, imperfect life. I fear I will never attain the holiness required of me in the Christian walk. The disquieting moods, vagaries, and disguises of my false self invariably interrupt, begging for forgiveness. The instant they come to my sentient awareness, I rest in Jesus who absolves them.

As I wait for God's completion of our family's story, I will continue to thrive in communion—not as one tendering advice but as a fellow traveler longing for what can never be fully realized this side of heaven.

When I awoke this morning, my first thoughts of the day were not spiritual ones. Clearing away the cobwebs from a night of erratic sleep, faith seemed like a distant dream, indistinguishable from the rhymes and rhythms of subconscious longing. Only those things I could see, touch, hear, or smell appeared real to me at this point.

Slowly, I began the process that gets repeated every day—that of turning my temporal mind in a more spiritual direction. With my prayers for the day at least begun, I reached for my journal and began to pen my latest reoccurring dream.

July 2018:

Sitting in a valley with a narrow sliver of stream running through it, I watch the sun, high in the heavens, cast a pale, silvery glow on the horizon.

My pulse quickens as Jesus approaches from a distant hill. Sitting beside me, He turns to ask, "Gail, what is your deepest sorrow?"

Tears, like droplets of grace in a baptismal font, fall onto my hands.

I say that my greatest sorrow is being so late in understanding
   his goodness.

I hand him a tattered scrap of paper, on it the words of St. Julian.

My fingers tingle, and I feel the full effect of God's purpose for
   me from all of eternity.

He releases every stain of guilt and tempest-tossed memory
   over a lifetime,

as my burdens fall effortlessly away.

Steve, Michael, Mom, and Dad come over to join us. Embracing, we dance in timeless synchronicity. As I fall into a deep pearl
of light, I'm filled with St. Julian's awareness that "All shall be well,
and all manner of thing shall be well."

I invite all interested readers to contribute to the
Selden Smith foundation for Holocaust education at
http://foundationforholocausteducation.org

Bibliography

"A Portrait of Jewish Americans." *Polling and Analysis* (blog), *Pew Research Center*, October 1, 2013, https://www.pewforum.org/2013/10/01/jewish-american-beliefs-attitudes-culture-survey/.

Adler, Mortimer J. *Truth in Religion: The Plurality of Religions and the Unity of Truth*. 1st edition. New York: Scribner's Sons, 1990.

Averill, Esther. *The Fire Cat*. Reprint edition. New York: HarperCollins, 2016.

Berger, Peter L. *A Rumor of Angels: Modern Society and the Rediscovery of the Supernatural*. 1st edition. Garden City, NY: Anchor, 1970.

———. *Questions of Faith*. 1st edition. Malden, MA: Blackwell, 2003.

Berkovits, Eliezer. *Faith After the Holocaust*. 1st edition. New York: KTAV Publishing House, 1973.

Bernstein, A. James. *Surprised by Christ: My Journey From Judaism to Orthodox Christianity*. 1st edition. Ben Lomond, CA: Conciliar Press Ministries, 2008.

Branover, Herman, and Ruvin Ferber. "The Concept of Absolute Time in Science and Jewish Thought." http://ldolphin.org/jtime.html.

Buber, Martin. *Two Types of Faith*. 1st edition. Syracuse: Syracuse University Press, 2003.

Camus, Albert. *Modern Classics Myth Of Sisyphus*. New edition. Harmondsworth, England: Penguin, 1975.

Carmichael, Amy. *Gold Cord: The Story of a Fellowship*. First edition. London: SPCK, 1932.

Carroll, Lewis. *Through the Looking Glass*. Scotts Valley, CA: CreateSpace, 2012.

Coelho, Paulo. *The Alchemist*. Anniversary edition. San Francisco: HarperOne, 2014.

"Einstein on Classifications." *Archives* (blog), *The New York Times*, February 16, 1930, https://www.nytimes.com/1930/02/16/archives/einstein-on-classifications.html.

Eliot, T. S. "The Giddings." In *Four Quartets*, 59. New York: Harcourt, Brace, 1943.

Ellena, Eric and Berna Huebner, dirs. *I Remember Better When I Paint*. Montreuil, France and Highland Park, IL: French Connection Films and Hilgos Foundation, 2009.

Ellis, Mark. "Five Myths about Christians' Support for Israel." *End Times* (blog), *God Reports*, May 12, 2014, http://godreports.com/2014/05/five-myths-about-christians-support-for-israel/.

Frethheim, Terence E. *The Suffering of God: An Old Testament Perspective*. Philadelphia: Fortress, 1984.

Freud, Sigmund, and Peter Gay. *The Future of an Illusion*. Edited by James Strachey. Standard edition. New York: Norton, 1989.

Friedman, Maurice S. *Martin Buber: The Life of Dialogue*. 4th edition. London: Routledge, 2002.

Friedman, Thomas L., and Special to the *New York Times*. "The Beirut Massacre: The Four Days." *Archives* (blog), *The New York Times*, September 26, 1982, https://www.nytimes.com/1982/09/26/world/the-beirut-massacre-the-four-days.html.

Frunză, Sandu. "Aspects of the Connection between Judaism and Christianity in Franz Rosenzweig's Philosophy." *Journal for the Study of Religions and Ideologies* 6 (2007) 181–205.

Frymer-Kensky, Tikva. *Christianity In Jewish Terms*. Reprint edition. Boulder, CO; Oxford: Basic Books, 2002.

Glenn, Susan A., and Naomi B. Sokoloff, eds. *Boundaries of Jewish Identity*. Seattle: University of Washington Press, 2010.

Goldman, Judy. *Losing My Sister: A Memoir*. Winston-Salem, NC: John F. Blair, 2012.

Greenberg, Eric. "Jews Affirmed in Their Wait for Messiah." http://www.bereanpublishers.com/berean/Cults/The%20Roman%20Catholic%20Church/Debating%20the%20Messiah.htm.

Greene, Graham. *The End of the Affair*. New York: Open Road Integrated Media, 2018.

Hallie, Philip P. *Lest Innocent Blood Be Shed: The Story of the Village of Le Chambon and How Goodness Happened There*. 1st edition. New York: Harper Perennial, 1994.

"The Hebrew v. Greek World View." *Teachings* (blog), *Torah Life Ministry*, accessed May 10, 2019, https://torahlifeministry.com/teachings/articles/23-bible-study/65-the-hebrew-v-greek-world-view.html.

Herberg, Will. "Rosenzweig's 'Judaism of Personal Existence':A Third Way Between Orthodoxy and Modernism." *Articles* (blog) *Commentary*, December 1950, https://www.commentarymagazine.com/articles/rosenzweigs-judaism-of-personal-existencea-third-way-between-orthodoxy-and-modernism/.

"Herman Melville (a Poem) by W.H. Auden." *Christopher Volpe* (blog), December 6, 2016, http://christophervolpe.blogspot.com/2016/12/herman-melville-poem-by-wh-auden.html.

Heschel, Abraham J. *The Insecurity of Freedom: Essays on Human Existence*. 1st edition. New York: Farrar, Straus and Giroux, 1966.

Heschel, Abraham Joshua. *God in Search of Man : A Philosophy of Judaism*. Reprint edition. New York: Farrar, Straus and Giroux, 1976.

Hill, S. J. *Enjoying God: Experiencing the Love of Your Heavenly Father*. Lake Mary, FL: Charisma House, 2012.

Hoffmeier, James K. "Out of Egypt." *Biblical Archaeology Review* 33 (February 2007) 30–41.

"Homily of His Holiness John Paul II." *John Paul II* (blog), *The Holy See*, accessed May 9, 2019, https://w2.vatican.va/content/john-paul-ii/en/homilies/1979/documents/hf_jp-ii_hom_19790607_polonia-brzezinka.html.

Kepnes, Steven. "'Turn Us to You and We Shall Return': Original Sin, Atonement, and Redemption in Jewish Terms." In *Christianity In Jewish Terms*, edited by Tikva Frymer-Kensky, 464. Boulder, CO: Westview Press, 2002.

Kimelman, Reuven. "The Theology of Abraham Joshua Heschel." *Issues Archive* (blog), *First Things*, December 2009, https://www.firstthings.com/article/2009/12/the-theology-of-abraham-joshua-heschel.

Kirov, Blago. *George Bernard Shaw: Quotes and Facts*. First edition. N.p.: n.p., 2014. Kindle.

Lakoff, George. "In Politics, Progressives Need to Frame Their Values." *Political* (blog), *George Lakoff*, November 29, 2014, https://georgelakoff.com/2014/11/29/george-lakoff-in-politics-progressives-need-to-frame-their-values/.

Lapide, Pinchas, and Karl Rahner. *Encountering Jesus—Encountering Judaism: A Dialogue.* New York: Crossroad, 1987.

Law, Sally. "The Exchange: Tony Hiss on Deep Travel," *Page-Turner* (blog), *The New Yorker*, November 14, 2010, https://www.newyorker.com/books/page-turner/the-exchange-tony-hiss-on-deep-travel.

"Learning Why Hadassah Hospital Was Nominated for The Nobel Peace Prize and about the New Hadassah Hospital Tower." *News* (blog), *Hadassah International*, accessed May 6, 2019, http://hadassahinternational.org/learning-hadassah-hospital-nominated-nobel-peace-prize-new-hadassah-hospital-tower/.

Levine, Amy-Jill. *The Misunderstood Jew: The Church and the Scandal of the Jewish Jesus.* Reprint edition. San Francisco: HarperOne, 2007.

Lewis, C. S. *Mere Christianity*. New York: MacMillan, 1952.

———. *Reflections on the Psalms*. 1st American edition. New York: Harcourt, Brace, 1958.

Lomas, Tim. "Self-Transcendence Through Shared Suffering: An Intersubjective Theory of Compassion." *The Journal of Transpersonal Psychology* 47 (2015) 168–87.

Lustiger, Cardinal Jean-Marie. *The Promise*. Grand Rapids: Eerdmans, 2007.

Magid, Shaul. *Hasidism Incarnate: Hasidism, Christianity, and the Construction of Modern Judaism*. 1st edition. Stanford: Stanford University Press, 2014.

Magnus, Shulamit. "Good Bad Jews: Converts, Conversion, and Boundary Redrawing in Modern Russian Jewry—Notes toward a New Category." In *Boundaries of Jewish Identity*, edited by Susan A. Glenn and Naomi B. Sokoloff, 240. Seattle: University of Washington Press, 2010.

Milgrom, Jacob. *The JPS Torah Commentary: Numbers*. 1st edition. Philadelphia: The Jewish Publication Society, 2003.

Moberly, R. W. L. "Knowing God and Knowing About God: Martin Buber's Two Types of Faith Revisited." *Scottish Journal of Theology* 65 (2012) 402–20.

Moltmann, Jurgen. *The Crucified God*. Anniv. edition. Minneapolis: Fortress, 2015.

Moore, Ryan. "Walking Far From Home, Part 2: Beauty and Pain on the Journey." *Blog* (blog), *A Sacred Journey*, March 13, 2013, https://www.asacredjourney.net/pilgrim-in-residence-ryan-moore-part-two/.

Neusner, Jacob. "My Argument with the Pope." Opinion (blog), *The Jerusalem Post*, May 29, 2007, https://www.jpost.com/Opinion/Op-Ed-Contributors/My-argument-with-the-pope.

———. *Rabbi Talks with Jesus, A*. First edition-stated edition. New York: Doubleday, 1993.

———. "The Implications of the Holocaust." *The Journal of Religion* 53 (1973) 293–308.

Nin, Anais. *The Quotable Anais Nin: 365 Quotations with Citations*. Edited by Paul Herron. N.p.: Sky Blue Press, 2014.

"Offering the Presidency of Israel to Albert Einstein." *Albert Einstein* (blog), *Jewish Virtual Library*, accessed May 10, 2019, https://www.jewishvirtuallibrary.org/offering-the-presidency-of-israel-to-albert-einstein.

Olson, Bruce, and James L. Lund. *Bruchko And The Motilone Miracle: How Bruce Olson Brought a Stone Age South American Tribe into the 21st Century*. Annotated edition edition. Lake Mary, FL: Charisma House, 2006.

Palatnik, Mrs. Lori. "Leah and the Lesson of Gratitude." *Aish.com*, January 22, 2000, https://www.aish.com/48945526.html.

Patai, Raphael. *The Messiah Texts: Jewish Legends of Three Thousand Years*. Detroit, MI: Wayne State University Press, 1988.

Pressfield, Steven. *The War of Art: Break Through the Blocks and Win Your Inner Creative Battles*. Edited by Shawn Coyne. 47716th edition. New York: Pressfield, Steven, 2012.

Rambo, Lewis R. "Theories of Conversion: Understanding and Interpreting Religious Change." *Social Compass* 46 (September 1999) 259–71. https://doi.org/10.1177/003776899046003003.

Remnick, David. *The Devil Problem: And Other True Stories*. New York: Vintage, 1997.

Sacks, Jonathan. *The Dignity of Difference: How to Avoid the Clash of Civilizations*. 2nd edition. New York; London: Continuum, 2003.

Shapiro, Edward S. "The Decline and Rise of Secular Judaism." *First Things: A Monthly Journal of Religion & Public Life* (March 2014) 41–46.

Shapiro, Gary. "'Over the Rainbow': The Story Behind the Song of the Century." *Arts* (blog), *Columbia News*, November 15, 2017, https://news.columbia.edu/news/over-rainbow-story-behind-song-century.

Shapiro, Marc B. "Maimonides' Thirteen Principles: The Last Word in Jewish Theology?" *The Torah U-Madda Journal* 4 (1993) 187–242.

Silberman, Charles E. *A Certain People: American Jews and Their Lives Today*. Softcover edition. New York: Summit Books, 1985.

Smith, Homer William. *Man and His Gods*. 1st edition. Boston: Little, Brown, 1952.

Stein, Edith. *Life in a Jewish Family: Edith Stein—An Autobiography*. Translated by Josephine Koeppel. Washington, DC: ICS Publications, 1999.

Stern, Karl. *The Pillar of Fire*. New York: Harcourt, Brace, 1951.

Tolkien, J. R. R. *The Return of the King: Being The Third Part of the Lord of the Rings*. Reprint, subsequent edition. Boston: Houghton Mifflin, 1988.

Tournier, Paul. *Guilt and Grace: A Psychological Study*. San Francisco: HarperCollins, 1982.

Tukey, Ann. "Notes on Involuntary Memory in Proust." *The French Review* 42 (1969) 395–402.

Unamuno, Miguel de. *Tragic Sense of Life*. Dover edition. Translated by J. E. Crawford Fitch. New York: Dover Publications, 1954.

Voskamp, Ann. *One Thousand Gifts: A Dare to Live Fully Right Where You Are*. Grand Rapids: Zondervan, 2010.

Weil, Simone. *Awaiting God: A New Translation of Attente de Dieu and Lettre a Un Religieux*. 2nd edition. Scotts Valley, CA: CreateSpace, 2013.

Wein, Berel. *Triumph of Survival: The Story of the Jews in the Modern Era 1650-1990*. First edition. Brooklyn: Mesorah Publications, 1990.

"What is EMDR Therapy?" *Resources* (blog), *EMDR International Association*, accessed May 10, 2019, https://www.emdria.org/page/emdr_therapy.

Wiesel, Elie. *The Trial of God*. 1st edition. New York: Random House, 1979.

Wiesel, Elie, and Marion Wiesel. *Night: With a New Preface by the Author*. New York: Hill and Wang, 1972.

Williams, Margery. *The Velveteen Rabbit: Or How Toys Become Real*. Reprint edition. New York: Grosset & Dunlap, 1987.

Wolfson, Elliot. "Messianism in the Christian Kabbalah of Johann Kemper." *The Journal of Scriptural Reasoning* 1 (August 2001). http://jsr.shanti.virginia.edu/back-issues/volume-1-no-1-august-2001-mysticism-and-scriptural-reasoning-messianism-and-fulfillment/messianism-in-the-christian-kabbalah-of-johann-kemper/.

Wolfson, Elliot R. "The Body in the Text: A Kabbalistic Theory of Embodiment." *The Jewish Quarterly Review* 95 (2005) 479–500.

Yancey, Philip. *Where Is God When It Hurts?* Anniversary edition. Grand Rapids: Zondervan, 2002.

Young, Joel, and Christine Adamec. *When Your Adult Child Breaks Your Heart: Coping with Mental Illness, Substance Abuse, And the Problems That Tear Families Apart.* First edition. Guilford, CT: Lyons Press, 2013.

Zondervan. *1001 Quotations That Connect: Timeless Wisdom for Preaching, Teaching, and Writing.* Edited by Craig Brian Larson and Brian Lowery. Pap/Cdr edition. Grand Rapids: Zondervan, 2009.

CPSIA information can be obtained
at www.ICGtesting.com
Printed in the USA
BVHW041256301019
562479BV00012B/75/P